This Joy That I Have
Life After the Storm

Shoner Johnson

This Joy That I Have: Life After the Storm

Copyright © 2017 Shoner Johnson

Words Matter Publishing

P. O. Box 531

Salem, Il 62881

www.wordsmatterpublishing.com

Published in the United States of America

ISBN 13: 978-1-947072-24-4
ISBN 10: 1-947072-24-2

Library of Congress Catalog Card Number: 2017938649

DEDICATION

M om, I will always cherish and love you. You told me to step out in faith and put myself out there. You believed I could, so I did! Watching you fight, grow, pray, hope, trust, and believe, when all of the odds were against you, made me believe in the power of miracles. You are a miracle, I honor you now and always. Your loving baby girl!

TABLE OF CONTENTS

FOREWORD

In my book *If It Had Not Been*, I told how my life changed when I found out my husband of 10 years had passed away.

My husband was so much more to me than a husband. He was a father figure to me. He was my protector, my provider, and my priest. I found myself when he found me.

I am the woman I am today because of his unconditional investment of love into me. When he passed away, I needed an outlet for my pain. I knew in sharing my journey with other people it would help ease my pain because I would be helping someone else that's exactly what my husband would have wanted me to do.

My purpose was birthed through my pain, indeed one of the most painful experiences of my life. I had no idea that the most painful time of my life, the place where I felt the lowest, the place where I felt like I was in a valley all alone, would be where I would give birth to my destiny and my life would never be the same.

Now, in *This Joy That I Have* I am sharing how your most painful times, your I want to give up times, your I feel alone times, and your times when you don't believe in yourself, are the exact times that you have been positioned for a life-changing experience that allows you to give birth to your destiny.

This Joy That I Have is not about the destination it's all about the journey. Your journey through this book will show you that no matter how deep you are, no matter how low you are, no matter where you've been or where you feel you're going. If you take the time to invest in yourself, maximum joy can be yours, and it can change your life forever and help you give birth to a beautiful life full of meaning. The very thing you thought was meant to destroy you, will create something so beautiful inside of you that it can't be described by words. *This Joy That I Have* will help you create and maintain a life of maximum joy and soulfulness, which will help you to have your best life in spite of everything that was meant to destroy. I want you to know there is joy available to you.

PROLOGUE

O ften in life, there is a paradigm shift that changes the trajectory of our destiny forever. Sometimes, we create our own paradigm shift either through a concerted effort because we want something different in life and we are seeking to change our life for the better or poor choices in life, which change our life dramatically for the worse. Sometimes, however, a paradigm shift comes unknowingly and unexpectedly. It can come when we least expect it. It can come when we have been lulled into a false sense of superiority over that which created us. We tell ourselves that we are the masters of our own destinies. Are we? Or are we not? Are we in total control? We'd like to think so, but our paradigm shift can be a stark reminder of just how frail and powerless we are. It is when a hurricane comes into our lives sucking us into its powerful epicenter of 110 miles per hour winds and thrusts us back out, to a different place that we learn just how weak we are. When we land in the midst of pure chaos, and total uncertainty, into a place that is completely unfamiliar. A place that was never in our life's GPS System. It is that alteration of our lives that is a reminder to us of our human frailty and personal powerlessness over the time and circumstance in our lives.

My paradigm shift came when I least expected it. It came strong, cold, icy, and cruel. It came with a powerful forcefulness that uprooted me and sent me reeling and knocked me into another place in my reality. It came to let me know, that which I thought I had power over, actually came to overpower me, and change the trajectory of my destiny forever. I would find out what it meant to have a life changing experience that would forever be a game-changer and come to a crossroad to face what I thought my life was and the reality of what my life was about to become. I would find out just what I was made for and the strength and power I had within to take that life-changing experience that was handed to me to create a brand new stronger more powerful definition of the woman I was at the core of my being. That paradigm shift would be the most powerful shift in changing the trajectory of my destiny forever. I would never be the same again.

What I found out from that experience was that a happily ever after does not exist. Our happily ever after is the work we do on a daily basis to create and maintain a life of joy in addition to or in spite of what has happened in our lives. The journey I'm about to take you on will help you create and maintain a life of joy and soulfulness in spite of what you have gone through or are going through. I want you to have your best life no matter what your circumstances have been or are now. The best of your days are still ahead of you. You can start today, creating a life of joy and soulfulness.

CHAPTER 1
THE EYE OF THE STORM

My happily ever after ended when my husband had a stroke and passed away, and I was left to pick up the pieces of my life with four children under the age of 12. That was my paradigm shift. That was my reality check that happily ever after does not exist unless I create my own joy. I lost my best friend, husband, priest, protector, provider, problem solver, prayer partner, and father to my children. Now, I would have to be mom and dad to my children. In one moment I was thrust into the center of an epic hurricane called life with no life vest or survival kit. I had no compass to guide me to the shores of safety. I was in the boat and had to find my own way back to shore.

Rebuilding my life after the loss was not an easy task. I found out that the rebuilding process is a marathon, not a sprint. I didn't know how daunting the process would be or how much work it would require from me emotionally, financially, physically, and spiritually. I did not realize how much it would change me at the core of my being. I did, however, come to discover who I am and where I want to go. Now, I am able to inspire others by sharing my journey and the lessons learned along the way. I took the time to create a life of joy and soulfulness. My pain gave me purpose. It gave me the desire to educate, empower, and encourage others to live their best life. A life filled with more than enough joy, more than enough love, and more than enough peace to create and have the life you want.

Where do you start in creating that life when you have gone through a transition in life? The first thing is to allow yourself the time you need to process what you are going through or have gone through to heal. You need to experience the pain, accept it, and allow that pain to heal you. This is the time to accept the reality of your life and live in that moment. This is the time to do some soul searching and get into yourself and listen from your soul. Be honest with yourself about what your reality is.

Be 100% true to yourself and where you are in your life. If you cannot be real with yourself, you can never grow and become a better person and live your best life. I know it's painful to look at our reality and face it. It's difficult to accept that the life we desire is not what we have at this moment. However, you cannot live in denial and move forward. I didn't want to accept my reality, but continuing to ignore it and sweep it under the rug and not deal with it, would have kept me stuck in a place where I didn't want to be. Open yourself up to the pain and allow it to heal you and change you. It will make you a much stronger version of who you are at your core.

Do you really want to spend the next five, ten, or twenty years stuck in a place in your life you don't want to be? Don't allow yourself to be stuck in pain, stuck in despair, stuck in a dead-end job, stuck in a bad relationship, or stuck in your thinking and not do something to change it. The power lies within you. You are the one to pick up the pieces of your life and move forward. Don't give your power away. Wherever there is life, there is hope. I encourage you to reach deep inside of you at your core and open up your soul and find the survivor in there and work hard to nourish that person to grow and become powerful and strong.

Pain is uncomfortable and renders us weaker than we normally are. But sometimes, that's what we need to heal. My son is a football player and one day during a football game, he tore his ACL in his knee. When we went to the doctor, the doctor said he would need surgery and physical therapy would be necessary to repair it. He had to go into my son's knee and repair the damage

This was a painful process and took a long time to heal, but it was necessary for him to be whole again. After the surgery, he was much weaker than he was going into it, but after some time resting and staying off of his knee and going to physical therapy and working on it several times a week, he became stronger and stronger until he no longer needed crutches or a knee brace. He was better and stronger. It's the same with us. Sometimes going through the pain is necessary for us to be whole again. But just like my son's surgery, we are going to have to do the work on a consistent basis to no longer need crutches and be able to walk whole again. Once you get that and work on that, you are in the best place to start your joy journey.

Whenever you face a loss or go through a major life change, your support system will help you through. They will be your life rope or your life line. Develop your support system around you. Your support system may be your family, friends, coworkers, neighbors, a Facebook group, or a support group in your community. Many cities now have groups in the city to connect people with common interests. People meet for coffee, networking, single parent support, a host of other hobbies and activities.

Your network should be people who are trustworthy, reliable, stable, and committed to you, your healing, and your success. It should be people who have your best interest at heart.

At times, we can be so proud; we think we don't need other people. We are erroneous in that thinking. By the very nature of our creation, we were created to thrive with companionship. Aloneness goes against the way we were designed. We all need people in our lives for support. We were created to be a we and not just a me.

So many people are despondent, depressed, and in despair, because they have not tapped into their support system. It breaks my heart to hear of people who give up and give in when they are overwhelmed. So many people in their deepest moment of despair take their lives because the pain is overwhelming. I knew I needed help. I understood I couldn't do it by myself. I utilized my support system, and that helped me each day to create balance in my life. I knew who to call if I felt overwhelmed, sad, or frustrated. I knew they would always be there for me and support me in any way they could.

Creating a support system for my children and me helped me to create a life of balance and joy. Each day became easier, each burden lighter, each trial easier to bear. The process of healing for me came with four people attached to it. So, it wasn't just about how I would move forward, it was about how we would move forward together as a family. We all needed healing, love, support, and encouragement. My children at the time were each in different stages of their lives, and they had different needs. My youngest three were in elementary school, and my oldest was in middle school. Her needs were very different from their needs.

My job was to figure out their needs and how to best meet their needs. Focusing on our whole family was much easier than meeting the individual needs at the time. The whole of our family was addressed first in my choice of careers. I knew, I had to choose a career that would allow me to be there for my children. My career at the time was very demanding and required extensive time away from my family, and the commute was far from my home. That was my way of creating joy and balance in my life.

When you are going through any kind of change in your life, find out what works for you. Each person and each family are different. Some people are blessed to have parents living with them who can help them with their needs. Some families are all in the same town, and you have a support system that can be more hands on.

Your primary goal when dealing with loss or change is to create a life that works for you and can increase your joy and soulfulness. No one has the right to dictate what works for you if they are not financially supporting you. We are the only people who have to live with the life we create. Also, no one can tell you how to grieve, cope or move on with your life after you've gone through loss or a major life change and the pain associated with that unless that person is a licensed therapist or life coach that you are seeking help from. If you need help from a professional get the help, you need to help you cope and to find peace and joy again. God created people with the ability to help us cope with life. Sometimes, we need medicine, therapy, group support, or personal counseling for an extended period of time to help us manage our pain and grief and that is why God created these things. Do what helps you cope and don't let anyone else dictate what that should be. As long as you are coping in a positive way and a way that won't harm you or others.

Don't ever forget, you are powerful, not powerless! My entire book is dedicated to helping you reclaim your joy after loss or change and to rebuilding your life. You and you alone are responsible for your joy and no one else. Do not allow anyone to judge your journey. Take ownership of your joy. Take your power back and work on maintaining your power throughout your life.

CHAPTER 2
LIFE ON PURPOSE

I believe to have the life you want, you must be purposeful in creating it. You must create a vision and create a plan to implement that vision. I maintain a vision board. On my vision board, I have the life that I am creating and the life that I desire to have. You have to envision where you see yourself and create goals short-term and long-term to get there. You must take ownership of your life and ask yourself the difficult questions. I had the desire to take the time to see what I wanted to do with my life and where I wanted to go with my life. My first challenge after my storm was to figure out how I could be a provider for my family and create a life for us. It was a huge amount of pressure to know you have four children depending on you for their sole survival and nurturing. If I didn't give it to them, they wouldn't have it. If I didn't provide, they would go without.

At the time of my husband's passing, I was asked the same question several times. Are you going to move back to Arkansas to be closer to your family? Are you going to move back to New York and live near you family there? In both states,

I had a very strong support system. I made the decision then that I thought was in the best interest of my family at the time, which was to stay put. I understood it would be harder because my support system was in other states. I knew, however, that in the long run, it would be beneficial for my children to stay, so we did.

My children had just lost their father. I couldn't move and have them lose their home, friends, school, church and any sense of stability that they had. I wanted as much of their lives to stay the same as possible so their journey to healing would be easier and less traumatic for them. I wanted as little disruption in their lives as possible and looking back on my decision, it was one of the best decisions I have ever made. Every decision made to move forward in your life will have to be made in the best interest of what feels right and organic for you. Whatever that decision is, if it helps you create and maintain joy in your life and doesn't cause anyone else pain, then it's the right decision.

It's difficult after being tossed around in a hurricane or tornado to come out and say, yes, this is how I will rebuild my life. When we go through trauma, there are stages in the recovery process and each stage is different for each person. Most people stay in a state of shock for a long time. When I went through my storm, I was in that stage for a while. I was able to function, but not live. I went through the motions to help my children cope and help ease their pain. Soon, however, I had to deal with my own pain and try to heal and move forward.

Often times, situations can make us feel powerless. When I had to rebuild my life, there were many times, I felt overwhelmed, but I had to remind myself, that the soul work

I must do to reclaim my joy is within my power. I wanted to be my children's role model for picking up the pieces of life when tragedy hit even though I was broken and bruised myself, I knew one day I would be healed and whole again, and they would see me walk that process out. They were my driving force for victory, for living a soulful and joy filled life. I couldn't help them become whole if I remained broken. My strength and power lay in the way I moved forward. For my children and me, I wanted to make the right choices. We may have been broken, but we didn't have to stay that way. I went through a personal and huge identity crisis. For most of my adult life, I was a wife and a mother. I was no longer a wife, but still a mother. My plans included being a wife and mother, enjoying vacations, anniversaries, graduations, and birthdays with my husband right there by my side. Oh, some of those things were going to still happen, but without him there. But the most painful part was some of those things would never happen again for us ever. I had to find myself and help my children blossom into who they were destined to be. What a monumental task for one person. I had to realize, it was a day to day walk.

Moving forward started with me going back to school to work on earning a second degree in early childhood education so I could become an educator. At the time of my husband's passing, I was on leave of absence from corporate America. Going back to corporate America and raising four children was not something I felt I wanted to do. I wanted to be able to be there for my children, and because most of my family lived out of state, I couldn't depend on my family members to help me. The choice afforded me the best of both worlds. I could teach and transform the lives of children and at the same time provide for the needs of my own children in a way that allowed me to be consistently present and active.

For a while, it worked really well, but as they got older, it became more difficult. My children started having several after school activities like cheerleading, gymnastics, football, basketball, track, and soccer. Our days were a lot less predictable as time went on. It was times like these; it would have been helpful to have my support system close to me. It was some of the hardest days of my life. So many times, I wanted to give up and give in. I didn't feel strong enough to handle it all. But, I had to remember, who I was and what I was to my children. That along with much prayer kept me going.

Each day was different, and each child's needs were different. Each day brought its joys as well as its challenges. My children were normal, typical children. They fought over nothing constantly. They thrived on annoying each other daily. They argued over who looked at who, who left the room first and lost their right to watch their favorite TV show, who touched who, who stared at who, who touched the other person's absolute favorite toy. At any given time they were immature, bossy, selfish, territorial, mean, and insensitive. Sound familiar? Each day, we worked on how to get along and respect each other and not make unkind choices. Things like this may interrupt your joy, but remember it's in your power to maintain it or give it away. I had to choose daily to maintain it despite whatever I may have had to go on in my life. I repeat, it was the hardest time in my life, and so many times, I failed my children by not being my best self. I was often reminded of the need to do soul work on myself to be strong enough to handle what I had been given.

I had to learn to navigate their lives and help them navigate their own lives as well. My goal was to create a peaceful, loving, harmonious family home where we all felt loved, appreciated, and respected. To say that, it was a difficult task to undertake would be an understatement. I had to establish parameters, rules of respect, and ways of disciplining my children that were effective. Sometimes it worked and sometimes it didn't. I didn't always get it right. My children have made me very aware of that. However, one routine my husband and I created was to have dinner at the dinner table each night. At each meal, we were able to share about our day. Each person had a chance to speak and be heard.

Also, each child had to come to the table with a Bible verse, a compliment for someone at the table, and one thing they were grateful for. This helped them learn to have an appreciation for what they had, gratefulness to God, and love for their siblings. As they have grown older, I can see the benefit of this time spent together. I share this with others who have young families because it's a great way to build a solid foundation for your children.

Studies show that families who eat meals together at the family table have children who do better in school and have a healthier self-esteem. They feel connected to a positive, harmonious unit. I can say with certainty that is true. My children did well in school and turned out to be loving, kind, successful adults.

There were times when I would get tired. It was a part of my life. Sometimes I didn't want to be mom and dad that day. I just wanted to come home, eat dinner, bathe, and go to bed. However, when I would wake up in the morning and see my sweet angels sleeping and hear the quiet stillness of a brand new morning, I had joy. I was grateful for my life and my journey. My story reveals to you my achievements, failures, trials, and triumphs. I'm thankful for it all because it has brought me to where I am today. After reading my story, I want you to feel empowered to rebuild your life after your storm and create a life of joy.

One of the best things I did for myself during that time other than creating a support system was to journal each day. Journaling helped me to write down my thoughts and feelings and helped me process my emotions. I was able to reflect on a lot of things and plan for where I wanted to go in my life. That's where I was able to write my vision down for my future and write down a plan with which to implement that dream. I was able to create goals for myself and for my children. Studies show journaling helps people heal emotionally especially people who are dealing with serious illnesses. There is something cathartic about getting your feelings and emotions out and letting go of the pain or lack of peace that you have. Journaling reduces stress, lowers your blood pressure and gives you more of a sense of appreciation and gratitude for your life, whatever your life may be at the time.

When you go through a change or loss in your life or seeking to change your life, it can be beneficial to keep a journal. Journaling helps you cope with the things in your life that are difficult for you and are keeping you from experiencing joy. As I journaled, I could look back on decisions I made and mistakes I made, and it helped me to see where I was at in my life and where I was going in my life. Journaling helped me to do the soul work necessary to lead a productive life and find satisfaction in my life.

As you go through the storm, as I have done on many occasions, allow that storm to strengthen who you are at your core. Dig deep within yourself to find strength and purpose. It's so difficult to be in that place because, at the time, we only want to get through it and put it behind us. I've talked to people who have said to me, I wish I would have kept a journal of my experience when I was going through my storm. There are things I wish I did remember about my experience. I love to journal because it is a release for me. It is a way for me to express so much of what's inside of me in a safe place and it is a mirror for me to go back to see where I was emotionally or mentally at different points in my life. It is a place I can go to and reflect on how much I have grown and how much God has done for me. I can glean wisdom from those writings and examine or reflect on why I made certain decisions or why I thought a certain way. It's an invaluable source of wisdom and information for us to learn from and grow from. Even if you are not a person, who likes to write, maybe you can keep a video diary. You can video tape you thoughts and feelings and play those video tapes back and see the growth in your life. These diaries could be valuable sources of information to the generation after you. There is always value in your Valley experience if you seek out the value. If you ask yourself, what purpose can I get from this? How can I use this experience for my benefit?

If journaling doesn't work for you, it's ok. Maybe there is something else that does. You may find gardening, singing, exercising, writing poetry, golfing, hiking, or some other activity brings you that same feeling of release and peace.

Whatever it is, embrace it and utilize it to bring you fulfillment in your journey and make you feel joyful and soulful. This is your soul work.

The third step is to create an action plan. When you create your vision, create your action plan to achieve your vision. Now here's the catch, you have to dream so big that for you to have your joy filled life, God Himself will have to bring it to pass. What do I mean? I have dreams so big that I understand, I can't accomplish them on my own. My strength, resources, time, and talents are not sufficient to accomplish my extraordinary life, so I'm clear that it will only be accomplished through God. My faith is so big that I believe he will send me the strength, time, talent, and resources to accomplish every dream He has placed inside of my heart.

I wrote down what I wanted to accomplish. I shared my dream with a few trusted friends, I knew would pray for me, encourage me, and hold me accountable to not give up, but persevere daily towards my goals. I started with baby steps, and I am allowing His grace and mercy to provide the rest. My vision plan included doing the soul work necessary to find wholeness and joy.

What is soul work? Soul work is the work we each must do to live our best lives. Soul work is the journey to discovering our true self at our core. It is the discovery of our values, longings, desires, and our truth and so I began my journey for myself to become my best self and fulfill my potential to live my best life.

Soul work helps us learn ourselves and grow as individuals to become our best self and have the most joy possible. It allows us to take the time to learn what gives us that soul satisfaction. Soul work takes time. It's a process. It requires us to spend time alone with ourselves to learn ourselves. We must spend time in prayer, meditating, and alone time to find our peace in self. Soul work requires disconnecting to reconnect. It requires disconnecting from noise, the noise of work, family, friends, social media, technology, and anything else that has the ability to interrupt our thought process. It requires intense amounts of time in peace and solitude.

If we don't do the soul work, we spend our lives going through the motions. We spend our lives existing but not really living. We spend time finding replacements for soul satisfaction. We find our value in things and not self. So what do we do? We shop, smoke, eat, drink, do drugs, hurt others, or hurt ourselves. Why? We haven't taken the time do our soul work. When we haven't done that, we attach other value to things that are physical or even worse other people.

We fill our closets with clothes and shoes because when our closets are filled with clothes and shoes, we feel valuable. We feel validated. When that gets old, we replace them with new shoes and clothes because we have to constantly upgrade our value. We go from relationship to relationship. We are always looking for that filler to fill the void in our life. It's a vicious cycle that will not stop because we haven't done our soul work. When was the last time you have done your soul work?

Spend time alone. Get to know yourself. (Do you know who you are at your core?) How much alone time do you spend with yourself? Spending time with yourself is the only way you can focus on developing and growing at your core. When you are alone, pray often and practice meditation. Meditation is a time when you are quiet and still and can focus on hearing the voice of God. In practicing meditation, learn to release and receive. When you sit with your palms face down, you are releasing all things toxic in your life. You are releasing anger, frustration, bitterness, unforgiveness, lack, depression, hurt, pain, or confusion. When you sit with your palms up, you are in the position of receiving, joy, peace, forgiveness, increase, focus, and prosperity. Practice deep breathing and learning to inhale and exhale.

Do this at a time, you know, you will not be interrupted. For me, early mornings work best. Read a scripture each day or read a positive affirmation to strengthen your faith walk and give you wisdom for life. Powerful affirmations strengthen us and increase our value and self-worth. Start attending church each week where you feel spiritually well nurtured. Start a gratitude journal, where you write 10 things you are grateful for each day. Practicing the act of thankfulness puts our minds in a more positive space. Space where we are more appreciative of the life, we have each day.

As you practice this in your life, it is my hope that you will slowly see, the change from within helping you feel healthier and whole again. I understand it's difficult to juggle it all in the midst of living your life, but it's the soul work you do that eases the pain and lessen the stress.

It will actually give you a happier, healthier, longer life. You will be stronger, better, wiser, and experience more joy as a result. Be ready to come out of your comfort zone. Be ready for that which is unfamiliar.

It's called the road less traveled.

- Have you ever taken the road less traveled or have you always stayed on the beaten path?

- Have you challenged yourself and come out of your comfort zone?

- Have you dared to be different even, if different meant unpopular?

- Have you ever been curious about what is waiting for you down that unbeaten path?

- Could it be a new career?

- Could it be a new adventure?

- Could it be the book, DVD, poem, business, or invention God placed in your spirit?

I enjoy taking the road less traveled. I took a vacation by myself to a place I had never been before. It was scary, exciting, and new. It was different. It was unlike anything I had done before. I knew no one there. I had no one to talk to or to spend time with. You know what? I loved every minute of it. I learned something new about me. I learned that I am more courageous than I thought. I learned I'm stronger than I thought. I learned that coming out of my comfort zone and taking the road less traveled allowed me to live my life OUT LOUD! It allowed me to be with me, learn me, hear my inner voice, and search my soul for an understanding of who I would become as this new single woman .

Now, I look for the road less traveled. I try new things and dreams new dreams. There are projects I'm working on that will take me out of my comfort zone. It's scary but exciting. I don't know the outcome, but I've come too far to turn back now. I have no regrets! I'm creating my best joy-filled life possible.

The faith to make a major step in one's life is not easily done. My hope is that you will have the faith and strength to make a concrete decision to take the road less traveled. It does not take courage to stay in our comfort zone, it takes courage to step out and choose our destiny. We can't complain about that which we refuse to change. We can't remain stagnant and expect to grow. Change is scary but necessary. It's difficult but important. It's imperative to your future and your future generations that you dare to be different. Live your life out loud!

Learn what gives you power and purpose and pursue that. Take the road less traveled and allow your destiny to unfold as a woman/man who left a legacy of courage to pursue the best life possible, unafraid and unapologetic.

It's never too late to start. Each day we are given is a new opportunity to try something new and do something different. Working on self-growth is the best thing we can do for ourselves and those we love. I did the work for my children and for me. I know I am a role model for my children. I want my children to respect me and make great choices for their life. This experience was new, but I lived it and did the best I could with it each day. I wanted my children to understand that life goes on after a loss. We have to learn to pick up the pieces and keep moving forward. I wanted to leave them a roadmap for how to move forward after a loss because I didn't have a roadmap. I had on the job experience and learned by trial and error. I was taken on a road less traveled and had to embrace it and leave footprints on the path as a warrior leader who took risks and overcame a difficult situation and not only survived but truly lived.

CHAPTER 3
TO THINE OWN SELF BE TRUE

Learning to live again for me also meant finding the faith to move forward in life and open myself up to love again. It had been about a year since my husband passed away and I was ready to open myself up to find companionship.

I had to think about where I was in my life and what was best for my children and me at that time. I had to ask myself was I ready to date again and why did I want to date again? Was I thinking about doing this for the right reasons? Because I was clear that marriage is a ministry and when you sign up for it, you have to be of the mindset that, your life is going from me to we, I knew I had to be sure I was ready. What I knew, from experience, marriage was not about me, but about my partner and me becoming one and having a single-minded vision for having the best life together, so we could fulfill God's assignment for us.

So many things were running through my mind. It was scary to think about bringing someone into my life. Who could I trust? How would I meet someone? Fortunately, I had a great support system around me, and everyone understood my need for companionship. God created us to desire companionship. I know, my late husband would not have wanted me to spend the rest of my life alone and lonely. He would have wanted me to meet someone nice and someone who could be a positive part of our children's lives. I was only 35 years old and was still very young to be a widow. I didn't know anyone else who was widowed so young.

I thought at the time I was ready for this new journey, In retrospect, I don't think I was ready. I don't think at that point, I had done enough soul work. I had not spent enough time rediscovering my true self at my core. I was trying to create a life free from grief at that point. I was trying to find what our new normal was. I desired that companionship to help me heal. I wanted someone to be there for me to hold me, love me, comfort me, and tell me everything would be okay. I wanted someone, who every now and then would let me hang up my superwoman cape and be soft, feminine, and vulnerable in a safe place. I wanted a partner that would let me exhale and be a strong shoulder for me to lean on every once in a while.

Trying to define what is normal is different for everyone. My normal was having a safe, happy, healthy environment for my children to grow and thrive. So, at that time, I hadn't done a lot of soul work. My soul works up to that point was trying to feel whole again and healed from the pain and grief of losing someone I loved. Now, I was going through the process of opening myself up to love again. Loving when I had no children was easy. Finding love or letting love find me with four children is totally different. I wanted balance. I wanted a mommy life and a Shoner life.

I did start dating again, and I was in for a very shocking reality check. Nothing was the same as it had been before meeting my husband. Everything had changed. I soon found out just how not ready I was. How would I know who to trust and who not to trust? I didn't know what to expect. Before children, I would have my date come to my house and pick me up.

Now, I couldn't do that so I would have to make sure I dated someone who understood, He could not come to my home. We would have to meet at the location of our date. I wanted to meet someone who was kind, loving, a Christian, stable, honest, and loved children. I desired to not just date, but to hopefully meet someone who could be a life partner and we could blend our families and raise our children together. That is something that is easier said than done. Looking back, I think that experience alone forced me to do a lot of soul work and find out who I was at my core and what I valued and deemed important in my life. It was a part of my soul work journey to finding and maintaining a lifetime of joy. The saying goes to thine own self, be true. How can you be true to a self you don't fully know and understand? My advice now to Christian singles who desire to minister in marriage would be to allow God to send the right person to you. Surrender yourself and your desires to God and allow Him to send the right person into your life. He doesn't make mistakes. He knows what you need and who you need in your life. Just focus on living your life in as meaningful a way as possible, and God will take care of the rest. I wasted a lot of time with the wrong people and had I just refocused my priorities, I could have saved time, energy, and emotions.

Creating a fulfilling personal life was more of a challenge, than when I was dating before. My perspective going into dating was with purity of heart and intentions. I wanted to date, so I could fall in love and get married. We all know love is a powerful drug! I had that drug before, and I wanted it again. I wanted to feel the experience of being on a love high with someone wonderful who wanted the same thing.

Many people, however, do not have a purity of heart and intentions. My desire was to meet someone who could grow to become my soul mate. I'm a relational person and find great satisfaction in being in a monogamous, committed relationship. I enjoyed being married, and I enjoyed the role of a wife. My desire was to have that experience again with someone who had the same goals and desires. Someone who believed that teamwork makes the dream work and that two are better than one and that a threefold cord is not easily broken. That was my desire and honestly speaking is still my desire. However, I believe it will happen in God's divine order of timing. He has definitely made me grow in the area of patience and understanding. He could have desired for me to work on parenting and my education at the time instead of dating.

What I have been able to do is gain a sense of self. I know what I desire in a mate. I've learned that trust has to be earned and should not be freely given and believe it or not a lot of people have a problem with that. I came to my place of understanding of what I needed and what my new reality was through a series of lessons learned throughout my journey. I learned, there was no replacement for the husband I lost. I learned some people have hidden agendas and you have to come to know that agenda through experience and spending time with that person. Now, I know how to discern a person's motive and character in a lot shorter period of time. I'm wiser now, and I can trust my intuition better. I've learned to listen to that voice of wisdom in my spirit that discerns things with precision.

My wisdom in this area came at a high cost and the cost often times was a painful price I had to pay. I would encourage all people to protect your heart and life at all times. Be very selective of who you allow into your life. My mistake was I listened to my heart and not my mind. The word of God tells us in Jeremiah 17:9, "The heart is deceitful above all things and beyond cure. Who can understand it?" Through life experience, I've learned not to trust my heart, but to trust the voice of the spirit inside of me because it will never steer me wrong. What I have learned is that, if it doesn't feel like God, sound like God, and act like God, it's not God. God is not the author of confusion. If you are in a relationship with a bunch of confusion and drama, which I was, it is not a relationship, God designed for you to be in.

I encourage you as much as possible to only allow like-minded people into your life and heart. The word of God says in Amos 3:3, "How can two walk together unless they agree?" This means that you should agree on goals, purpose, children, spiritual lives, finances, etc. When you are getting to know someone, spend a lot of time talking. You will soon find out if you are of a like mind and can walk together in agreement.

When you allow someone to open up to you through conversation and get to know that person, sooner than later they will reveal who they are at their core. At the time, I started dating again; I was caught up in my feelings and emotions. I wanted to get married, and I wanted it to happen in my time. I was willing to rush into getting to know someone and take what they said at face value. I would see red flags, but ignore them because I wanted what I wanted. This is an example of my not taking the time to do the soul work necessary to know and understand self and to value myself, so much that I would not allow anyone in my life that was not meant to be there.

You will learn how to do this when you have done the soul work necessary to understand yourself. When you learn who you are and what you want, you can weed out the imposters quickly. I hope that through my journey to joy, from my failures and experiences, you can glean from my wisdom and not pay such a high cost. Some of the things you may want for yourself, God may not want for you. Always trust the still small voice of the Spirit inside of you. It will always lead you to that which is for your highest and greatest good. It will lead you to your divine place of joy, peace, and tranquility. In my joy journey, I have met many people. The people I met came into my life for a reason, season, or lifetime. Each person I allowed in changed me in some way. I received more of an understanding of myself. I trust God more now than I did then. I learned about the depth of His love for me through my immature decision making and impulsivity. His grace and mercy through those times helped me through the pain of my disappointment in myself. My joy now comes from a place of grace, thankfulness, and mercy. I am able to extend the same grace and mercy to others, God extends to me.

One of the best pieces of advice I could give to people who are on a sincere journey to create and maintain a life filled with joy would be to take the time to get to know you. Joy comes from knowing who you are and embracing the totality of your knowing. You are able to become comfortable in your own skin. Even through adversity, you can still find joy.

I was going through a really difficult time one day. Everything that could go wrong did. I was losing my joy. I was beginning to see the glass as half empty, not half full. I was tired and discouraged. I remember walking into a dark room. It was so ironic because it was symbolic of my dark mood and outlook at that moment.

However, when I walked into the room, there was a single point of light in that room. The television was the only point of light in the room. As I looked at the television, it was on the nature channel. The channel was showing scenes from nature along with soft soothing music. It was showing waterfalls, beaches, sunsets, deserts, and rivers with flowing water. As I sat down in my chair, feeling stressed, tired, weak, and discouraged, it was as if, God completely washed me in one of those waterfalls because I felt a wave of peace flow over my entire body and everything negative or discouraging left me at that moment.

I felt completely refreshed, relaxed, and at peace. I didn't remember how long I sat there watching that channel, but it was exactly what I needed at the moment I needed it. I was able to find joy during a difficult time. That day, I felt the presence of God in that room, and it felt so good. These are the ways, we can hold on through difficult times, seeking moments to bask in the presence and peace of God.

CHAPTER 4
THE POINT OF IT ALL

Seek to see each life experience as an opportunity for growth. There are extremely painful experiences that we all go through. Let that experience grow you. When you're praying to God and seeking peace from God, truly seek to hear and understand as His spirit speaks to you. Often times we speak, but don't take the time to hear and understand. The ability to be still and listen in the midst of pain is quite challenging. The voice of our pain cries so loudly that it drowns out the still small voice of comfort. It is true, however, that the voice of God indeed speaks through pain, fear, uncertainty, and anxiety. Can we listen and if we listen and He does not respond the way we think He should, or His response is silence? Are we able to accept it? We must trust His divine wisdom and have peace with it.

- Ask yourself these questions.

- Do I allow my negative experiences to make me better or bitter?

- What was your last negative experience?

- How did you respond to it?

- Was your last experience a loss of a job or relationship? How did you react?

I challenge you to think about the moment. Think about what happened at the moment you experienced that. Was your reaction fear, hurt, anger, tears, yelling, or shock? When the moment was over what did you do about it? Our reaction can change the trajectory of our future.

Let's use for an example getting laid off or fired. What would you do at that moment? What would you do after the moment had passed? Anything that causes deep feelings or emotions in us impacts us for a long period of time. If you were laid off or fired, now you face the challenge of how you respond to it. In our human nature we would be hurt and angry, but at some point, we must push forward. How we push forward is the key to creating and maintaining a life of joy and soulfulness.

I have a very dear friend, who after many years of faithful service to her career and being highly esteemed by her colleagues as very competent, was suddenly faced with a possible layoff from a seemingly secure company. Her future with the company was in jeopardy, and she could have been facing a very difficult financial future. Her impending layoff was shocking and scary. She could have had many different responses to her experience. Her response was to utilize the experience to sharpen her career skill set and work smarter at making herself an indispensable asset to the company she worked for. Not only did she not get laid off, but three short years later, she has been promoted to one of the most esteemed and prestigious positions in the company and is making more income than she ever has in her life. She became better and not bitter. She used her experience to maximize her potential and in return, she was rewarded with a dream position at her company. Our negative experiences are designed to bring something out of us or pour something into us. It is human nature to feel negative emotions when something happens to us through no fault of our own. We have to challenge ourselves not to remain in those emotions or use those emotions to effect positive change.

What if, your negative experience is from a failed relationship? A relationship that you gave your all to and despite that, it still didn't work out? The person did not appreciate your presence in his/her life and didn't see you for the gift that you were to him/her? Maybe they cheated on you or emotionally, physically, or financially abused you. You knew you were a diamond, but the wrong Gemologist did not see your worth. Are you allowing the person who caused you hurt to grow your character or stunt your character? Do you see yourself as a victim or a victor? How did you respond? After that experience was over how did you heal and what did you learn about yourself? Did you do any soul work to help you heal? It's truly not about that person when it's all said and done. It's about you. I have learned so much about myself from those experiences. I've learned there was something inside of me that was flawed. Something that needed healing and was broken. I will never allow anyone that type of power over me.

I had to do my soul work when my relationship failed. I had to work on me and my role in it. I believed there was potential for a fulfilling relationship with this individual so, I allowed this person into my life and into my heart. I asked myself what could I have done differently, but at the time, that is why I made the decision to move forward with this person. I had a desire to give love and receive love and be in love with a great person. I asked myself, what lesson did I get from this experience and what I can do differently next time to not let the wrong person into my life? Allowing the wrong person in can be a waste of time for you and delay your journey to your life of joy. I had to reflect on me and what was going on inside of me at that time. There was something lacking inside of me that needed to be developed and matured to be able to clearly discern the motives of people early before I involve my heart and emotions. I challenged myself, and I grew as a result of the soul work I did. This is the importance of knowing yourself and setting standards for you and not accepting anything less and praying to God and asking for discernment in important life decisions and when you pray and ask God for an answer, and it's not the answer you want, leave it in God's hands. Don't act like you didn't hear God and you keep praying hoping He changes His mind and gives you the answer you want.

Now, through my own soul journey, I can discern motives whether pure or deceitful early on into meeting someone. Our intuition is there to lead and guide us. Trust your intuition and always proceed with caution, but don't ever be afraid to love hard in spite of a broken heart because it may make you miss out on the best ride of your life.

Don't be afraid to ask as many questions as necessary in the beginning to know that person. Choose dates that allow for conversation. Places where you can talk to each other and be open with each other. The more time you spend talking, in the beginning, the better because you will truly get to know this person you are considering allowing into your heart. That is a very special place for someone to be, protect it and cherish it.

Many times, we use placebos in place of the real healing to help us get over a negative situation in our lives. Some people's placebo is jumping from relationship to relationship to get over the hurt from the past relationship and don't realize they are bringing compounded compacted hurt to each relationship and the new relationship has no chance of success because of all of the complicated layers one or both people may be bringing into the relationship. Two people are developing complicated soul ties to damaged individuals and the complicated soul ties you bring to each other is only destroying your joy and soulfulness and delaying your journey to your place of peace.

Other people may use work, alcohol, or drugs as a placebo. They truly believe the "medicine" they are taking will heal them of their wounds and don't even realize they have been taking a placebo the whole time and wonder why they are never healed. Nothing can take the place of doing the work necessary to move forward as a healed, whole person, with a stronger sense of self. Your layers you leave with should be layers of strength and wisdom, purpose, and sense of self.

Here are some more questions to ask. Do I believe God can show me more of Him through this experience? Can I see the character of God in this situation? Have I perfected the art of listening to the still small voice of the Spirit of God inside of me that will always lead me to the truth? If you have not asked yourself these questions and spent the time necessary to find the answers, you may be in a great position right now to move into a greater dimension of who you are.

I believe your experience is an opportunity for God to bring you closer to Him and understanding His purpose for your life. We can better understand the character of God through our most painful experiences. The beauty of it is that He can show Himself differently with each experience we are in. He has shown Himself differently to me with each new experience in my life. I didn't understand Him in the past as I do now.

Sometimes, God will give us the very thing we need for us to learn what we need to prepare us for a greater revelation of Him. There are many ways that He speaks to us. The power that comes from knowing He is speaking directly to you about your situation and showing you more of Him is priceless in our journey of joy.

Maybe, if you had not gone through that divorce, you would have never gone back to school for your law degree. Maybe, if you have not lost your job, you would not have started your own successful business and became as successful as you are. Maybe, if you had not lost your house in foreclosure, you would have never relocated and met your new husband/wife. Just maybe, it was allowed for a greater purpose. A purpose that may or may not be revealed to you at the time you are going through it. Sometimes, it's only revealed on the other side of through.

CHAPTER 5
BE STILL AND KNOW

Do you know your purpose? Do you have the ability to discern that which is for your highest and greatest good? Just because something is good doesn't mean it's for your highest and greatest good. The ability to discern that takes wisdom and experience. In youthful immaturity often times, you may have done something impulsively because at the time it seemed like a great idea. It was something you felt would bring you immediate gratification. As you grew and matured, however, you were less keen on making decisions based on impulsivity and immediate gratification. Through age, wisdom, and hopefully maturity, you have learned to be more deliberate about the decisions you make. This is the process by which you gain the ability to discern that which is for your highest and greatest good. The more introspective you are, the stronger your ability of discernment becomes. Get to know and understand yourself well. Your intuition and spirit guide you away from situations and people who are not designed to be a part of your journey because they are not for your highest and greatest good.

Have you perfected the art of listening to the still small voice of the Spirit of God inside of you that will always lead you to the truth? This is the spirit that will lead you to your highest and greatest good. Work on perfecting the listening process. Work on hearing the wisdom from within to lead you to decisions that will help you become happy, healthy, and whole. Our inner voice will speak truth to our lives. It will help us feel peaceful with our decisions. It will give us confidence with our choices. If your inner voice doesn't lead you to light, love, and positivity, work on building more positive thoughts inside of you and start surrounding yourself with like-minded, positive people and things.

Doing only that which is for your highest and greatest good will lead you to a purposeful life. I encourage you as much as you can to live your life on purpose. Don't let life happen to you. Be proactive in the decisions you make and the things you do. This includes weeding out all things and people who do not have a place in your destiny.

They may be great people, just not great for your master plan for your life. The sooner you realize that the sooner you can make the decision of whether or not they stay or go. I believe the reason so many relationships fail is that two incomplete people who have not done the necessary soul work to find out who they are and where they are going, and who do not have a sense of self, are trying to come together. Thus the relationship is based on superficial characteristics and not for the lasting purpose of walking together to accomplish their destiny and God-given assignments both individually and collectively. All of these factors add to the escalating rate of broken marriages leading to broken people trying to find wholeness and completion in that which can never truly make them whole.

If you are in a place in your life where you desire a relationship, ask yourself why do I desire this at this time? Am I ready for this? Do I know what I desire? Am I complete and whole? Can I identify a potential partner that is complete and whole? Do I know what my destiny is? What soul work do I need to do to get there? If I meet someone, what value do I bring to their life and what value do they bring to mine? Asking these questions and having the ability to clearly answer them will be key in moving forward with the right person at the right time for the right reasons.

When we are soulful, we tend to attract others that are soulful as well. If people come into my life that are not a true reflection of the beauty of God in my life, they don't stay long because it's been said and bears repeating, that light drives out darkness. I have learned to trust my gut. I don't want to waste my time or his time. So when someone leaves your life, either willingly or unwillingly, celebrate for yourself and them because it was not meant for the two of you to walk out your God-given destinies together. It doesn't necessarily mean anything negative other than, God has a different plan for both of you and that's a beautiful thing.

Also, if you are single, please proceed with caution. I believe, dating should be with the express purpose of finding a mate to marry. Too many people are living without purpose or intention. Too many people, men, and women are dating to feed their flesh and not dating to feed the soul and their life's purpose. Why waste your time or theirs? Why engage in a relationship after relationship only because it feeds your flesh and not your spirit. Some people get involved in a relationship strictly to feed their flesh, and they wonder why it doesn't end up working. Nothing born from the flesh will ever sustain you long term. It wasn't designed to and never will. True lifelong joy is not born in the flesh; it's born of the soul and spirit. I implore you to not live your life through your flesh and start living your life through your spirit and watch the change in the joy in your soul and spirit.

If you are married, you can ask yourself, how can my spouse and I do the soul work together and individually to both feel soulful and have a life of joy? A place where we can both work out our God-given destinies together? Do you plan date nights where you can bond with each other? Do you pray regularly with and for each other? Do you talk about goals and dreams together? Do you both have a master goal that you are working on together? Do you partner with other successful couples and support and encourage each other? Are you both worshipping in a congregation of believers that nurture you spiritually? Do you mentor younger couples and help guide them spiritually and emotionally? Do you read books together that will help you? You can read the Bible together, books on finance, books on creating lasting marriages, or books on how to become your best self. These are tools to bring you together and allow you to explore each other more and understand how your spouse thinks.

Through my life experience, soul work, and reflective thinking and through reading books on successful marriages, I've learned when you seek to add these strategies to your marriage; you will see the benefits to you and your spouse for a healthy, productive, successful, lasting marriage. Also, you will leave a powerful blueprint on your legacy. Your marriage will change the marriages of your children and your grandchildren. You will be the ancestor talked about for generations to come. These are the things that can help you live a life of joy and peace that will strengthen you and hold you through the uncertainty and difficulty that life can bring. My desire is to educate, empower, and encourage you to live your best life. Our best life comes when we live our life on purpose and often pray for guidance and direction. It is then we can see the fullness and fruitfulness of our lives. You can then celebrate and say, this joy that I have, the world didn't give it, and the world can't take it away.

A purposeful life is a productive life. Life after a loss can be just as fulfilling as life before the loss. When we experience a loss of any kind, it changes us permanently. We can still, however, find our purpose and live our lives with purpose. The loss is as much a part of life as living. The cycle of life is birth and death, however, painful it may be. Our greatest challenge is to find out the greater purpose behind our loss.

For me, the greater purpose behind my loss is to help others through transitions in their life and help them find their purpose. I found my purpose in writing and being an inspirational speaker. My gifts are being used to help others. I found that gift through my loss and being a mom to my children and using my gifts with them.

In raising my children, I focused on helping them find their gifts and talents. I sought to nurture those gifts and talents. My daughter said to me that growing up, what she appreciated most was I allowed them the opportunity to explore things that brought them joy and fulfillment, and I allowed them to change their mind.

My daughter played the saxophone for several years. She enjoyed it and was good at it. She played for several years but decided after several years, she wanted to do something different. I was not going to force her into something that no longer brought her joy. She would only experience success if she were gifted in it and passionate about it. This view has served me well in pursuing my passions and gifting of pouring life into other people.

Now that my children are adults, I parent them in a different way. My role has changed. My role as a mom has gone from the custodial parent, nurturer, and disciplinarian to mentor and life coach. I can now take all of my painful lessons; wisdom earned and learned, and turn them into purpose through helping my children. This is a part of my joy process.

I can maintain my joy and help my children get their joy, purpose, and passion too. Transitioning from mom to life coach was not an overnight transition for me or my children. Even now, they don't always accept me as their life coach and mentor. Children as teenagers and young adults are focused on creating their own identity apart from their parents.

They want to be their own individuals and create their own life path. They rely at times on peer approval and being accepted. My children like others, don't always take my advice. They don't always come to me for advice. A lot of times, they come to me after the fact, but at that point, the damage is done. Then they want mom to play clean up woman. They are metaphorically speaking broken and bruised. These are the times when my purpose becomes clear because it's my job as their mom to navigate them through these teachable moments and help them find meaning behind it. Often times the consequences they face can bring more value to the experience than my words ever can.

Sometimes, their lesson comes when they face the consequences of their own actions no matter how painful those consequences may be. As a mother, my job is not always to prevent them from feeling pain. Sometimes, they may need to feel that pain to understand, why they should not have made the decision they made. I was speaking with a dear friend of mine and we were discussing helping our children grow and mature as young adults. I said to her, as parents, there are a lot of things we can teach our children.

There is a lot of wisdom we can give them, but sometimes there are things God wants them to learn from Him, and that's why we will not be the ones to teach them that particular lesson about life. Sometimes they need to gain that God wisdom in their life to help them grow and mature as a person.

Your Joy is what you feel each day. Your joy is what you feed your soul. Your joy is what sustains you from day to day. Your joy is what is inside of you that radiates on the outside. Have you done a joy inventory? Have you sat down and focused on what brings you joy? Too often we are going through life in function mode. We function daily off of what we need to do. My joy inventory consists of all of the things that make me happy and feeds my soul. Some of those things are big, and some are small. I get joy from family vacations with my children. I get joy from family time at a restaurant or dinner table. I get joy from flowers, perfume, and chocolate. I get joy from all things outdoors, such as hiking, biking, swimming, laying on the beach, or enjoying a nice meal on an outdoor patio. I love looking at the stars on a clear summer night. That's when my imagination can run wild and take me to faraway places I dream of visiting one day. I get joy from accomplishing goals. I always have a goal in mind that I want to accomplish. I enjoyed working towards my degrees knowing, I will be able to care for my family.

When I earned my degree in education, and I started teaching, I took my sons out of their school and placed them in the school I was teaching at. Some people asked me if I minded having my sons with me all day every day at the same school. I didn't mind at all. I loved it.

I spent so much time away from them when I worked for corporate America. I relished the time we spent together. The school was far from my home, so we spent a lot of time in the car going to and from school. I had that quality time with them to talk about their day and have quality conversations with them. That time was precious to me, it brought joy to me. Also, there was a walking and biking trail down the block from my school. The trail is called Silver Comet Trail. It stretches from Georgia to Alabama. When the weather was nice, I would put their bikes in our van, and after school, I would run while they rode their bikes. Sometimes I would lace up my roller blades. It was a great way for them to get their energy out and for me to exercise and decompress. That was joy work that I was doing.

Do you have a joy ritual that you do? Are others a part of that joy ritual? The cliché is true. It's the little things that count. Each moment we spend creating joy is another opportunity to bless the people in your life that you love, that's why having a life of joy is critical. The people you love benefit just as much as you. Your joy fullness and soulfulness can change the very atmosphere of the room you walk into. The part of your joy that is manifested can help others as well. I have a family member who gets tremendous joy in helping others. I had frequent gatherings at my house when I lived in New York. I would invite her over often to my gatherings. She would always come over and celebrate with my family. Every time she came, she brought her joy with her. By nature, she is a very helpful person. So, when she would come over before she would leave each time, she would clean and wash dishes, and the kitchen would be spotless when she left. I really enjoyed her helping me so much. I appreciated not having to do any cleaning after she left, but sometimes I felt guilty for allowing her to work so much.

One time I had a Christening for my son. I invited her over but told her she didn't have to do any cleaning. Just come and enjoy the party. Well, she came over and did just as I requested, but it wasn't the same. She didn't seem to get that much joy out of the experience this time and that, in turn, made me feel bad. I had stopped her from doing the very thing that gave her joy. Her joy came from helping others. It was her gifting. She was excellent at it too. After that, I allowed her to help anytime she wanted too. I enjoyed the help, and she enjoyed helping. We are all different, what gives us joy is very different for each person.

My next joy journey was setting a goal to get my master's degree in education. I enjoyed my job and wanted to learn as much as I could to be the best teacher. I also wanted to earn more money to support my family. Coincidentally, getting my master's degree coincided with me turning 40. I decided to set several high goals for myself. I set goals that would help me feel joyful.

One goal was to run in my first race, so I signed up for the Peachtree Road Race. The race is 6.2 miles. At the time, I was not a runner, so I knew I had to start training. I also wanted to lose weight and be at my goal weight. I knew I had set the bar high. I would have to work full time, raise my children and meet their needs, train for the race, and maintain a healthy diet, so I could lose weight and work on my master's degree at the same time. Whew! That was a lot to put on one plate. Not to mention my children's extracurricular activities.

How did I do it? I sat down and wrote a plan of action. I wrote small weekly goals that I would accomplish each week. It was very beneficial to me because it helped me have a greater focus. I wasn't able to run 6.2 miles, so I started out just walking the whole route. Slowly, I built myself up to running. My children were a great support system. I shared my plans with them, and they supported me. I took small steps daily in accomplishing my goals.

When I turned 40, I had accomplished all of my goals. I completed my master's degree. I lost all of my extra weight and had competed in the Peachtree road race and was able to run the entire 6.2 miles in an hour and 17 minutes. Talk about feeling all the joy I could stand. The road wasn't easy. It was really challenging. There were times; I had to run in the rain. There were times I was so tired I cried myself to sleep. There were times, I was so frustrated with all of the responsibilities, I took my frustration out on my kids, but through it all, we made it together. They were there to cheer me on at the finish line of the Peachtree Road Race. They were there to cheer me on when I crossed the stage with my master's degree. My journey took a lot of commitment and dedication. It was tough because I was doing it as a single parent. Your journey to creating and maintaining the joy you want will come with challenges, setbacks, discouragement, a lot of sacrifice and lack of support at times, but it's so worth the journey. What price are you willing to pay? It's going to cost you for sure, but seeing your dreams come true, I'm sure is worth the price you will have to pay.

Have all of my dreams come true? No. Have I become all that I hope to become? No. There are things that I desire that I still don't have. There are things I want to do and haven't done yet. In spite of that I keep dreaming, hoping, pushing, and pressing because one thing I know for sure, if I don't work for it and keep striving for it, I will never have it. If you knew you could not fail, what would you attempt to do? How would your life be different? Life is short and uncertain. Please maximize the short time, you have here on earth.

There will be many trials and tribulations that come in the way of your soul's satisfaction. There will be people and situations that take you clear off of the edge. Things happen. Situations change. Life happens. Life will at times get on your last nerve. You will get angry, heated, and feel overwhelmed. Sometimes you will feel like a thief has come and stolen your most prized possession, your peace. We are human. That's understandable. It won't feel fair because it won't be fair. It will, however, be an obstacle that you can overcome and use as fuel for your joy journey. When we overcome obstacles and setbacks, we appreciate our joy journey that much more.

I think the mistake that many of us make is we get

stuck in that setback or that obstacle. We don't pray enough for strength to get through. I promise you that when you go into your secret place to pray to truly get into the presence of the holy God things will change. When you are on your knees bowing before Him and praising Him with an open heart, mind, and soul, joy enters. At that very moment, in the presence of the Holy God, the atmosphere of the room changes and you fall on your face in thanksgiving because you feel the power of His presence. You feel your soul being filled to capacity, and everything you are going through is washed away in the thought and feeling of his love for you. All of the sadness, anger, regret, bitterness, longing, hurt, and betrayals leave your heart, mind, and spirit and He heals all of your hurts and touches you in your wounded place gently, but powerfully, reminding you of His deep and profound love for you. My God, can't you just feel His presence now?

Only our Devine Creator can bring us the satisfaction our souls long for. Why? Because He created our souls. He is the inventor and manufacturer. He wrote the instructional book on how His product (us) work. Don't let your setback keep you stuck in defeat. It will keep you in a state of lack. You will lack in joy and soulfulness. You are stronger than that. You were brought to it, to get through it and become a better person because of it. You are strong, brave, and capable. Don't give up and don't give in. Find a way to get through it that works for you in a healthy way.

Your healthy way could be yoga, prayer, worshipping at the church of your choice, exercise, hiking, biking, swimming, meditating, or seeing a professional therapist. Lean on your support network. Remember, you have the power to make your life a life of joy. Hard times come, but hard times go too. Joy really does come in the morning, however long that morning takes. Just hang on until your change comes. Encourage someone else who may be going through. They may need your strength to help them hold on. You may be a part of someone else's joy journey. Give selflessly and generously. No one is meant to go through their joy journey alone. We need other people to help us feel soulful. Other people can deposit in us, what we are lacking, but make sure those people are bringing you joy and not taking your joy. People can be joy snatchers. Discerning a person's role in your life is critical. The more you know and understand YOU, the more you can discern those who are there for the right reasons. I was blessed to have a wonderful system of supporters in place, friends, family, and my children kept me on the right track at all times. My children frustrated me and drove me nuts sometimes, but they also brought me the greatest amount of joy.

CHAPTER 6
STILL, I RISE

Have you ever seen a flower grow through a crack in a concrete sidewalk? I've seen a dandelion growing in a crack in a concrete sidewalk. It seemed weird to me. Why, because a dandelion's natural habitat is in the field with other dandelions, grasses, and plants. Did the dandelion choose to grow in between the cracks in the pavement? No, it did not get to choose where it was born and grew up. It had to grow in the place it was planted as a seed. The same is true for us. We did not get to choose the circumstances in which we were born. For many of us, we had to grow and live where we were born, and with the parent or parents, we were given. It always amazes me how in the midst of the most unlikely circumstances, a delicate flower can push through a crack in the concrete. Concrete is tough and difficult to break through. We use jackhammers to break through concrete because of its thickness and density. Yet, I have walked down the street and seen a small yellow delicate dandelion push through something that has the ability to crush it and grow tall, straight, and colorful and full of life despite the circumstances through which it was birthed. It grew through the crack in the concrete. It grew where it was planted. It found a way to survive. It found a way to bloom where it was planted even though its habitat was foreign. It grew there because that is where it was meant to grow. If it had fallen a few inches to the right or a few inches to the left, it would not have been born at all. It would have withered and died because it would have fallen onto the concrete and not in between the cracks in the concrete.

Do you see it now? You were born in the circumstances that you were because had you been born anywhere else or to anyone else, you would not be the person you are today. You might find yourself in a difficult circumstance with all of the odds seemingly stacked against you. You may have so much pressure on you; it would seem likely that you would be crushed. From the natural eye, you have no means of sustaining life under such pressure. You have no visible means of support. You are all alone in your circumstances just like that flower. To the visible eye, you are in a fragile state, and with the right amount of pressure, you can easily be crushed, just like the flower growing in the concrete. However, just like the flower. Little by little, slowly, you have pushed your way through that concrete. You were pushing through the black darkness that surrounded you. No one saw you pushing because it was so dark where you were. In that darkness, however, God was sustaining you, fertilizing you, giving you just the right amount of nutrients that you needed to give birth to your breakthrough, to give birth to your breakout. Nobody knew what was going on in your darkness, but there was movement. There was activity.

By all accounts, you shouldn't have been born at all. You survived being born under a layer of concrete. There is no sunlight, there is no life-giving oxygen to help you thrive. But you pushed through. You struggled. You persevered. You didn't give up, though. Inch by inch you continued to grow, trust, believe and receive from God just enough strength to continue forward. Slowly, you began to see the light of day, even when no one noticed you. They didn't know that you were in the process of being birthed out of your circumstances and about to push through your concrete barrier that has held you back so long. They didn't notice because it happened so slowly.

The more God nurtured you, fed you, encouraged you, the more you pushed up, higher and higher until you become visible again to the natural eye. Now when you finally burst forth in all of your glory, you are a beautiful representation of God's glory revealed in you. The more your glory is showing, the more your character is developing. The stronger and straighter you become. People are so enraptured by your beauty and your glory, and your magnificence; they don't even see the filth and dirt that you were just birthed under. They don't see the layers and layers of muck and dirt; you had to push through to get to where you are today. Despite our inability to choose our beginning, we can choose today our ending.

All they see is a beautiful reflection of God's glory revealed in your smile through the soul-full-ness inside of you. You know where you were birthed, and that's all that matters. You were meant to be here. You were meant to survive what was supposed to kill you. You were meant to live through it and come out victorious. You were meant to grow right where you were. You were meant to change lives, thrive, flourish, create companies, and create families and legacies all because you were born in the crack in the concrete sidewalk.

You were meant to be born in the crack of the concrete sidewalk because someone is in that crack behind you and they are about to give up, and they need you to reach down through all of the muck and mire that they are in. They need you to get your hands dirty and help pull them through that dark area. They are experiencing a shift, and they don't know what's going on. They are experiencing an uncomfortable season, and they need someone who understands the shift, who understands that flowers do grow in the crack in the concrete sidewalk and those flowers carry an intangible beauty that is theirs alone.

They don't see their beauty because it's so dark where they are. You, however, are there to assist in the shift. Because you know, the shift brings in the necessary light for them to start pushing up and out of their below-ground birthing canal. Each push and each pull carry with it more strength and more power. You are that push and that pull. Your strength is the difference. Your presence is the catalyst because you are that flower too. I am that flower. I am the person that wants to see you come out of your situation and grow and thrive.

Creating and maintaining a life of joy when your situation and circumstances dictate that you should fall apart is tough to do. Whatever you might have gone through or are going through, I feel your pain. I want to encourage you, in the midst of it, to see yourself healed and whole. It's difficult to do when the doctors have told you that you will never walk again, you have prostate cancer, or you have colon cancer or breast cancer. You may have a child pass away, or a child go to jail that you may never see again. These are seriously difficult circumstances that are painful to deal with. Life is often unfair, and it doesn't always reward us according to our goodness, but in spite of that, we must find our lesson and purpose in the midst of it.

I am convinced; we can acquire greater wisdom, greater value, and appreciation for life when we go through painful situations. I never felt like I took my beautiful marriage for granted, but when God decides it's my time to get married again, I will have a great respect for the blessing of marriage because of my years of being the head of household and sole provider for a family of five for so many years. It has been extremely difficult to manage a household of five all by myself. The responsibility of knowing, that if I don't provide, my children will suffer has not been easy. It has, however; created a stronger sense of appreciation, gratitude, humility, thankfulness, purpose, and joyfulness at all that God does for me each and every day. This, in turn, will make me better for my future husband. I believe God is perfecting me in areas where I am weak. My family will benefit from my pain and my growth. There is value in all that I have gone through, and that value will be a blessing to my children, my children's children, and to my future husband.

When I think of Olympic athletes or professional athletes, I think about all of the hard things they endure. They train all day every day for years and years. They sacrifice time with family and friends. They are constantly being pushed passed their comfort zone. Many times they face isolation for the sake of competition. They have days of pain, soreness, and fatigue. I'm sure there are days they want to give up because the emotional, mental, and physical cost is so much. There is no big crowd there cheering them on. There are no TV cameras and magazine covers. But despite that, each day, they get up again and again and do it all over. Because they understand all of the stretching, pain, fatigue, and soreness, will be worth the glory of winning a gold medal or winning a championship because that prize says they are the best in the entire world.

God requires the same of us. He wants us to be the best for His glory. When He is molding us into what He wants us to be. Whatever, our calling is, we go through a season of shaping, preparation, discomfort, isolation, hurt, and heartache, and humbling, but when we come through our season, we are at our best for His glory, and His glory will be perfected in us. His glory, when perfected in us, makes our joy that much sweeter. We know what our joy cost us and when we pay a high price for something, we value it more.

I asked myself when I see people overcome extreme obstacles, how they did it. How do people with extremely difficult challenges get through their challenges and inspire other people? I've seen cancer survivors inspire other people. I've seen double and quadruple amputees overcome their challenges and inspire others. I've seen homeless children attend and graduate from prestigious Ivy League universities.

How did they do it? How did they manage to overcome such extreme difficulties, beat the odds that were stacked against them, and not only succeed but use their story to inspire others to succeed in life as well? Do they have a magic secret? No, they have a determination to make their current life, their best life and create joy in the life they were given and share that joy with others. There was something inside of them that said, you are not supposed to be here. There is something greater than this for you. There is something better waiting for you, so go get it. Others have made a conscious decision each day, not to give up, but to keep pushing. Our passion gives us joy and creates a desire within us to share that joy with others.

You can create your own story of overcoming. Search for the meaning in your situation. Create joy despite what you are going through. Don't settle for getting by. Strive in your current situation for more than enough. More than enough joy, more than enough peace, more than enough purpose, more than enough perseverance, and more than enough strength to shine your light in your dark place. Your more than enough light will be a light and a blessing to those around you. It's a life circle that changes pain to purpose, trials to testimony, tears to triumphs, struggles to strength, and setbacks to success, all for God's glory and your peace.

How does pain produce purpose? Purpose comes from that which empowers you. By definition, the purpose itself is motivation, cause, occasion, reason, point, basis, or justification. We have a couple of choices when we experience pain in our lives. We can allow it to destroy us, the essence of who we are or we can allow it to build us. I have used my pain to help build me so I can be effective for the benefit of others. I have used my pain as a character builder and a teacher. Some of my pain was not caused by me, but truthfully, some of my pain came from my willful acts of disobedience to God. In each situation, I strived to learn, grow, stretch, pray, and move forward with what I have inside of me to become a better person.

When I think of pain as a useful feeling, I think of working out at the gym. I think of strength training with weights. When I work out with weights, I feel it. I feel my muscles tightening and burning. It hurts a lot. I don't like to feel that pain. I don't enjoy hurting. I feel it after my workout as well. I feel it two days later too! I feel sore. My muscles let me know, they are being stretched and pulled. However, I understand some pain is necessary for my muscles to grow strong and firm into the fit body that I want. For this reason, my pain has a purpose. The purpose is to help my body function properly and keep me healthy and strong.

Likewise, our life pain can produce purpose. Take for example someone who has a child who commits suicide. I cannot imagine the tremendous amount of pain that must be a parent. That has to be one of the most painful, heart-wrenching things a parent has to go through. Now the parent is faced with a choice. Give up or go on. Most parents choose to go on. Some of these parents go on to create support groups for other parents who have lost children as a result of suicide.

They go on to create non-profit organizations that go to schools and educate children about suicide prevention. So many other situations I can name where people have found purpose and that is what helps them to cope, grieve, and get their joy back. When you do this, you can feel that your soul is full, and your life has more meaning.

Earlier, I referenced turning trials into testimonies. Has your trial produced a testimony? Have you gotten through what you were going through or are you still going through? If you are out of your trial or storm what is your testimony? Have you encouraged someone else with your story? Can you reflect back on your trial and use it as a testimony? There is someone waiting on you. They are waiting for your story to inspire and encourage them. It will give them hope and comfort. Allow your trial to birth a testimony in you. Each of my painful experiences has produced an added chapter to my life story. I'm determined to use that life story as a testimony to encourage and inspire other people. We do not know whose life we will impact by sharing our struggle of overcoming in the face of life's difficult obstacles.

We have to be aware that the words we speak are powerful. We can change a person's thoughts and actions by the words we speak to them. I still don't understand some of the pain I have gone through. But, I have to remember, I've gone through it, and it's behind me. I'm no longer in it, which means I have come out victorious. Is my life over, No! Will I go through more pain, probably? Now, it's different. I have life experience that has shown me, just like the other times, I will get through this too. Just remind yourself like I did that this is just another chapter in your book. Just make sure your book is worth reading.

Setbacks to Success. I love reading a good comeback story. I love reading a story of how someone has overcome a setback and then achieved great success and accomplishments in their life. I'm always the one rooting for the underdog. I'm sensitive by nature, so I feel people's pain when they are going through difficulty, but I rejoice when I see them overcome. I love it because it inspires me. It shows me that God is no respecter of person. What he does for one, he can do for someone else. I use these stories as inspiration for me at moments when I need encouragement or motivation. We all have times when we face a setback and want to give up or throw in the towel. We may be making progress and going forward, then something happens, and we are thrown ten steps backward. It could be the loss of a job, marriage, health, or a loved one. At the time, it could feel like you are never going to recover. You feel like you are in the ocean and the minute you come up for air to breathe, you are pushed back down even farther, and you feel the pressure on your body on the inside, and it feels like you are going to explode. I know, I've been there several times! You just think I'm not going to survive this one. You can survive it, though, and you will survive it. As long as you are alive, there is hope! Where there is life, there is hope. Trust in God for everything and He will bring you through everything. He can give you peace that no one or nothing else can give you.

After your setbacks, prepare to make your comeback. Prepare to work harder than ever to see your dreams come true. Prepare to go to battle for the peace and soulfulness you desire in your life. Our journey is constantly changing and evolving, but we must be ready to change and evolve with it so we can have a meaningful life. I'm here to encourage you, and yes you can do it. You can have joy after the pain and joy after the rainfall of disruption in your life.

Look for people you know or research people you don't know, but have heard about who have overcome their own setbacks. I'm inspired by people like Tyler Perry, who went from sleeping in his car to half a billionaire all because he refused to give up or give in. He faced several setbacks and obstacles on his road to success. He never gave up believing in himself or his dream. I believe his setbacks were setups for his success. He is stronger, better, and wiser. He is helping hundreds of people with careers as a result of his success. He used all of his life experiences to help himself help others. I admire him for that. I would love to experience success in my life that will allow me to bless so many other people.

Did you know that Colonel Sanders had thirteen jobs before he experienced success with his restaurant business? Did you know, He was sixty-five when he opened his first Kentucky Fried Chicken restaurant? Ten years later, he had ten franchises he was operating at the age of 75. Wow! Talk about turning a setback into success. Delayed, but not denied, dreams do come true. Talk about it never being too late! We all know of countless stories of people who did not give up and were rewarded for their perseverance as a result.

From poverty to prosperity. From broken to a billionaire. From minus net worth to millionaire, nothing is impossible with God. It does not matter where you are right now. It doesn't matter how many degrees you have or how many connections you have. It doesn't matter that you never went to college or dropped out of high school. All you need is your belief in yourself and your faith in God to experience a life of joy and soulfulness. I believe by faith that my latter days will be greater than my former. I believe that I am destined for prosperity in my heart, mind, body, and soul. As I do the work necessary to fill my soul and have a joyful life, I know, that all of my needs will be met and some of my wants as well.

I don't have a poverty mentality. My mind is sound in the belief that God can and will do all things except fail. What stage are you at in your joy journey? Are you in the can do stage or the cannot stage? I'm in the can do stage. I'm thoroughly convinced I am on my way to my prosperity life.

Even when I encounter setbacks in the future, my life is blessed and will continue to be blessed. If I experience a setback, I will not experience a setback in my thinking. It will not detract from my soulfulness of body and mind.

The only way to rid yourself of a soullessness mentality is to wash yourself of it and do not go back to it. Think of it this way. Have you ever gotten mud on you? I have, and it doesn't feel good. Mud is dirty and makes us feel dirty. It's sticky and nasty. It could have germs and bacteria in it that are harmful to us. Well, the only way to rid yourself of mud is to get out of the mud, go wash yourself off with soap and water, put on clean clothes and don't go back to the mud again. Once you have the feeling of mud on you, you know what it feels like and don't want to have that feeling again. The same is true of our mindset. When we gain a mindset of joy and soulfulness, we don't want to go back to the emptiness of joylessness and soullessness. When we rid ourselves of negative thinking, people, habits, and proclivities, we feel cleaner, lighter, happier, more grounded, and soulful. Once we rid ourselves, why would we go back? Protect yourself with a passion. Be the gatekeeper of your joy.

Gatekeepers are trained to keep out anyone that might infiltrate the protected home inside. They are trained to sift out the dangerous and prevent it from coming in and causing harm.

Now you are the gatekeeper. It is your job to utilize the power of the Spirit to keep out the unnecessary and dangerous from your soul palace. Once you become trained, it's easier to detect an infiltrator. They have a certain way about them that alert your senses and tell you something is not quite right.

You know, they are up to no good, and they are there as a saboteur to your peace, joy, and wellbeing. When you know this, it's time to weed them out and send them on their way before they do damage.

CHAPTER 7
THE POWER OF NO

Here is another thought. Perfect the gift of subtraction. Yes, Subtraction! Subtraction is the letting go of anything that prolongs or deters you from your joyfulness and soulfulness. God has blessed me with many gifts. He has blessed us all with multiple gifts. One of my gifts is the ability to forgive others and love them despite the way they may have mistreated me. When we forgive others, move on, and love ourselves, it frees us to walk in the joy and fulfillment God has designed for us. It doesn't mean they are a part of my life anymore, but being angry with them doesn't hold me hostage anymore and allow the cancer of unforgiveness inside of me. I can forgive them and subtract them from my life and move on in joy.

When we practice the gift of subtraction, it allows God to bless us by addition and multiplication. I could decide not subtract from my life all of the hurt that I've gone through. I could hold on to all of the pain that people from my childhood caused me. I could hold on to the hurt from the betrayal of past relationships, I could hold on to the bitterness of friendships that ended in betrayal. I could hold on to anger at God for taking my husband and the father of my children away from me.

I'm sure there are people and situations in your life that you could think of right now, that have disappointed you, hurt you, abused you, missed you, took you for granted and neglected you. I want you to know this. You have every right to feel the way you do! Your feelings are valid. If your perception is these things happened, then that's your reality. I understand your pain. Let me encourage you beloved, today is your day to start subtracting.

Find the strength inside of you, and I know it's there. To start subtracting every negative feeling and emotion, you have inside of you about your past. Subtract the hurt, pain, disappointment, anger, resentment, neglect, shame, and fear. Decide today that you will do the soul work necessary to let it go!

I decided in my joy journey to start subtracting things from my life for God to increase others things in my life. I started subtracting disappointment about my past mistakes. I did it, I repented, it's over, so I let go. Gone! Done! I will not continue rehearsing the pain and disappointment of my past mistakes like scenes from a bad movie in my mind. It does nothing for my joy journey and can never make me feel soulful in my life. Done! I subtracted my resentment and anger of past relationships that did not work out for whatever reason. The constant remembering of them was an unnecessary waste of the valuable time God has given me here on Earth. Once again, it's over. Live, learn, and move one! I subtracted those feelings because I want all the joy I can stand and I need to make as much room as possible in my heart, mind, and spirit for God to add to and multiply my joy! I want my future husband to be attracted to my joy, love, peace, gratitude, and soulfulness. He cannot be attracted to that which is not there!

Are you ready for God to start multiplying in your life? Are you ready for multiplication using repeated addition? Great, you are on the right track. Now, start perfecting repeated subtraction in your life. Subtract all things from your past that rob you of your future.

What is it that you want God to multiply in your life, your finances, your career, your peace, your love, your joy, your mind, heart, body, or soul? Then today is the day to call the trash collector to come get rid of all the junk you've been keeping in your basement. Yes, the basement of your soul, the soul which guides your spirit and life to that which is for your greatest and highest good. Trust me, you won't be missing anything, and you will open up your heart, mind, and spirit to the joyfulness and soulfulness that you desire. God is going to multiply your joy so much; you will have all the joy you can stand.

It's time to start writing your past, a goodbye letter. It may go something like this.

Dear past,

Thank you for all the lessons learned. Thank you for all of the good memories. I won't hold the bad memories against you. I'll just erase them from my mind. Now, it's time for us to part. See, you just don't have a place in my future anymore. I will no longer allow you to hold me hostage by bringing up anything negative from you,

Relationships, mistakes, failures, and downright no good people. You have been stalking me for a long time now, and I'm tired of it. I will only move forward from here. And yes, this is personal, so take it that way. I'm moving on now, and I have a new love, it's called my future. I'm going to love it, hold it, nurture, it, and give it all that it needs to stay in my life. We have a good thing going on, see, I feed it joy, love, peace, thankfulness, and gratitude and in turn, it gives, me hope, light, faith, strength, and prosperity, peace, and love. It works very well for us.

Sincerely,

Happy and blessed.

Once you write that goodbye letter to your past, burn it forever to ashes from which it will never rise again. Once you say goodbye and move on, you are in prime position to receive that which God has for you. Do not let anyone bring your past up to you either. The minute someone tries to remind you of your past, stop them in their tracks and say, I've said goodbye to my past. I've changed addresses and no longer live there, and I didn't leave a forwarding address. If you want to go back to the past, you can go alone. You gain so much more in return by doing this and the people around you know, you are moving forward from your past. I'm gifted with forgiveness and love, and I feel free as a result.

I only surround myself with people who are like-minded. I'm a positive person, and I surround myself with positive progressive forward thinking people. Your destiny is shaped by the person you are and the people you surround yourself with. If you don't surround yourself with forward thinking people, how can you move forward? Don't surround yourself with people who cannot assist you in subtracting from your life. Take inventory of where they are. Have they been able to effectively subtract from their life? Or are they holding on to people and things that add a negative value to their life? The people and things you surround yourself with should not be subtracting from you. If so, it is, or they are no longer necessary.

Don't let another person talk you out of your destiny. Don't let another person block your blessing. Don't let another person tell you what you cannot do. Don't let another person tell you your dream is not possible or you don't have the right connections and people in your life. Reject every negative seed people try to plant in your life. Stop the negativity at the root of bitterness from where it came. You can and you will, I believe in you.

There are right people, right resources, right timing, and the right opportunities for all of your dreams to come true. If these weren't meant for you, God would have never put the dream inside of your spirit. These people are destiny killers and subtractors but in a negative way. They subtract from your hopes and your dreams, but they don't have the faith and courage to believe in their own hopes and dreams, so they try to block yours. Now, is your time to subtract these people from your life, so God can add people who will support, build, nurture, and believe in your dream. When you have vision and perseverance, and you don't compromise it by the flesh, it produces multiplication.

There are so many dreams I have and so many talents I want to put to use. I haven't tapped into all of the things I want to do, but I do know, if God put it in my spirit, it's a seed that He plans on nurturing until He sees it to fruition. I know it won't be easy, but it's possible. I'm nurturing those dreams now, and by the time you finish reading this book, I believe some of those dreams will have come true.

Seek to add value and seek to always be in a place of increase. Even if you don't have much, you can fill your life with increase. One of the best ways to increase your life is to surround yourself with knowledge. The public library is free, and there is a wealth of knowledge to be found there.

Make a new habit of reading books to improve your life and better yourself. Books teach us so many things and give us so much wisdom and knowledge. We can improve our life exponentially just by reading books that will help us grow as individuals. I read books in areas that I seek to learn more about. I want to be more knowledgeable in areas that will help me. I enjoy reading books on finance, exceptional living, and books on spirituality.

These books help me become a better me. They teach me to improve my life. The addition of books in our lives to gain a greater knowledge will be the increase we need to create and maintain a life of joyfulness and soulfulness.

As I stated earlier, Prayer is a powerful tool to use in adding the increase to our lives. Prayer is the key that will unlock so many doors in our lives. Our words have so much power. When we pray prayers of faith and thanksgiving, we are in a position to receive all that God has for us. Prayer helps in the building of our relationship with God. Prayers of praise and thanksgiving draw us closer to God and God closer to us. There is so much joy to be found in an effective prayer life. Prayer is the awesome time we spend with God letting Him know just how great we think He is. It is the intimate time that we spend with God developing our love relationship with Him and drawing strength from His power. He is the nurturer of our souls. Prayer is the resource that can fill our souls to capacity. The power of prayer unlocks the doors of joy and peace in our lives.

So many times, when I have been down, I spent time in prayer and worship to God letting Him know, how much I love and adore Him. The more I did this, the better I felt. The lighter my load seemed. When we get into our prayer closet, miracles start happening outside of our prayer closet. We are able to connect intimately with God, and He draws closer to us and wraps us in His love, power, and strength.

The enemy tries to battle us in our mind. He tries to stifle us through the thoughts in our minds, but when our mind stays on positive things, and we fill our lives with prayers of faith, that's when we have won the battle. We have the ability to take our thoughts captive and control the negative seeds that start to grow in our minds and debilitate us mentally. We become weaker in our spirit and stronger in our flesh, which is the opposite of what God wants for us. It is in direct opposition to His will.

God knows our heart and when we pray from our heart. He hears our prayers. We unlock the possibilities of our promises when we begin to pray by faith. When you pray, I hope you start declaring God's promises over your life. Start declaring what your future will be and when you pray believe what you are praying. Speak the powerful Word of God in your prayers and start declaring His promises to Him. Hold Him to His Word.

Start reminding yourself of your prayers when you face a difficult setback. Remind yourself that you are victorious, and you are in a season of increase in your life. Even when it feels like there is subtraction all around me, I know He is multiplying exactly what I need. He sees something I need to be added to my life. When I am down and discouraged and feel my joy leaving me, I remind myself of all of the wonderful promises of God in my life.

I know from reading the Bible that I am more than a conqueror through Christ Jesus. I know through my promises in God's word that I can do all things through Christ, who strengthens me. I know that it is God's good pleasure to give me the desires of my heart. I remind myself, I am able to have all that God desires for me. He wants me to have a great life and a light-filled life. I can have a life of prosperity and peace no matter what my circumstances.

People tell me, you are always smiling. Yes, I am, because this joy that I have the world didn't give it and the world cannot take it away. I am walking in the assurance that my latter days are greater than my former. I'm walking in assurance knowing; that the awesome life God has planned for me will far outshine the darker days of my past. I walk in the light of my victory knowing that the rest of my days will be the best of my days. When you know that and get it in your spirit, you too will walk around with a big smile on your face.

It is the confidence that people will see in you. The

confidence in knowing you are secure, protected, and well loved by God.

There is no secret or magical formula. It is well known and free to all. You will have what you think you will have. I think I am. Therefore I am. Once you have completed the subtraction phase of your life, you will see an abundant increase in all that you desire. You will experience the blessing of God's multiplication. Multiplication adds increase not just to you, but to those around you as well. Seek to multiply your intelligence and wisdom. This will take you far. Seek to increase your attitude of gratitude. Multiplying the nontangible things in our life will bring far more peace and joy than material things ever will.

Material things are great to have, and if you practice subtraction, you will receive an increase in the multiplication of material comforts in life that we all desire to have. I would love to have a fine home with fine cars in the driveway and a shoe closet that would satisfy all of my shoe fantasies. I love bling and would love to have a closet full of blingy things, shirts, shoes, dresses, and very blingy jewelry! Hey, I'm human. But the end result will be that all of that bling will become old and dated, and I will want to donate it to charity and purchase some new and updated blingy things, why? Because the bling can never satisfy my life's desire for joy and contentment. Your contentment can never be satiated through the material. How many celebrities are unhappy in multi-million dollar homes? How many celebrity divorces do we hear about constantly in the news? They are blessed with millions of dollars in the bank. Money is not satisfying them. It never will. Only having a joy filled soulful life can bring us what we desire the most, peace.

Self-love is the best love. The addition of the nonmaterial is the only sure fire way to guarantee that your joy is a lasting joy, A joy that will impact the lives of the people around you. They are going to want to get on your joy train. There is more than enough to go around. Don't you love the idea of being multiplied so much in your life, that you can share, and the supply never ends?

Maybe right now, it's tough to think about adding joy to your life because right now, you might be in the middle of the biggest battle of your life. I want you to know, this battle did not come to overtake you, but to make you stronger. You are not in this fight by yourself. God is right there by your side. If He brings you to it, He will bring you through it. He is the good Shepard, the Shepard that will lead you through your darkest night. He is the shepherd that will never leave you to be devoured by the wolves in your life around you. He has a measure of grace and mercy for you that are yours alone. He has a special anointing on your life that will carry you through your darkest hour. When you feel the press of the pressures of life, and you feel squeezed beyond your breaking point, remember you have everything you need to break free.

When I was in a season of God subtracting in my life, it was one of my darkest hours. I didn't see my joy, I didn't feel His hand leading me and guiding me. I didn't feel His peace that surpasses all understanding. In the midst of it all, all I could see was darkness and despair, but I didn't give up, and I didn't give in. I held on because I knew He would never leave me nor forsake me. I knew He would turn things around for my good. I encourage you today to let your joy come from a place of knowing. A place of knowing, that God is right there. God is multiplying in your life right now. He sees you, and He is saying, you need more of my love, so I'm going to shower you with my love.

The mistake we make is that in our moment of weakness when the pain is really intense, and it hurts so badly, we desire immediate relief, so we find an out for that moment. What can we do instead? We can cry out for his love to shower us and surround us, so we don't feel the intensity of the pain. We must reach inside of ourselves and seek to fill our soul because that will fill our hearts and minds. We must strive to become better than we are because when we become better than we are the whole world around us becomes better.

When God showers us with His love, we don't have to look for it because it's all around us and His love is inside of us. It leads us and guides us to that which is for our highest and greatest good. His love is a transforming love. If you open yourself to that love, it will enable you to become the being you were created to be. Be purposeful about opening up to seeing that love and feeling that love. Have you ever cried yourself to sleep and when you woke up the sun was shining so bright? That was God's love. Have you ever been so cast down you couldn't smile, and your child or grandchild came and gave you a hug? That's God's love. Have you ever had a coworker or friend speak the right word at the right time? That's God's love. You come home from work, and that's the day the kids are behaving, and all is going well at home? That's God's love. Maybe your spouse surprises you with flowers? That's God's love. You needed a financial blessing, and it came to you right on time, that's God's love. One Friday after I arrived at work, my coworker brought me breakfast. I felt loved and appreciated. So many times, I received unexpected checks in the mail when I desperately needed a financial blessing. That's God's love. So many times, I was struggling with an issue or a problem and God worked it out in such a magnificent way, He was the only person that could get credit for it. That's God's love. He shows Himself to us all the time, we just have to be able to recognize, that it is God showing us His love. To see that love, we must remain centered in our soul. We must do the work necessary to continuously fill our soul to capacity because when we are soul filled, it is easier for us to recognize the move of God in our lives.

The light at the end of a tunnel when you are going through a storm is that it will come to an end. Tell yourself, you are strong enough to endure this temporary place in your life. Because where you are is just that, a temporary place. A place you were not meant to stay at. A place you were meant to go through to get to. To get to that place, God desires for you, the place of promise where God wants you to be, your promised place of destiny you must have a desire to get there. It is the place on earth, where you will receive your joy, your peace, your love, your appreciation for what and who God has blessed you to become.

When your storm comes to an end, you will have a new appreciation for all of the things God multiplied in your life. Storms help us appreciate the brevity of life and the fragility of life. It helps us appreciate the rainbow after the rain. That understanding brings a stronger sense of value to our lives. We know what our life could be, so we are thankful for what our life is. The thankfulness is the joyfulness that we have and that in turns make us feel soulful. We appreciate our relationships more, families more, friendships more, children more, homes more, careers more, and the intangible gifts we have inside. It's not the perfect place, it's the perfect, for us, place!

CHAPTER 8
WISDOM OF THE AGES

It's not easy or cheap to cultivate a life of joy. My life of joy came at a price but, now I have the tools necessary to maintain what I have inside of me because I know the price I've paid to have it. The joyfulness we have comes with maturity and experiencing life. It comes from our life experience and the life experience of your elders who share their wisdom with you. We are then required in turn to share that wisdom with others. It would be a travesty to glean wisdom from our lives and the lives of our elders and throw it away like a piece of trash or put away only to be forgotten about. There is no value in that. Also, the travesty is we will inevitably repeat the same poor choices and have the same difficult life experiences and watch our next generation after us, go through the same pain and shame because we did not grab, value, and hold dear to the wisdom, we had available to us. Wisdom comes to us to help us make better choices, get to our destiny faster, and help others along the way.

My mom is not just my mom, best friend, and confidant; she is also my spiritual mentor. She is one of the wisest people I know. She is always reading, studying, watching, learning, and listening. She watches the news, reads newspapers, books, magazines, she watches talk shows and all of the news stations, and religious programming. She loves to learn new information. She is literally a wealth of knowledge. She always knows just the right things to say to me to make me feel better. She always has the right perspective I need on how to handle difficult situations or important life decisions. She tells me always seek to do right and God will take care of you. I know God speaks to me so many times through my mom because I feel His spirit inside of her. She has seen a lot and experienced a lot and all of that wisdom and life experience, she shares with me freely, and as a result, I have made some great choices in life and have been able to forgo a lot of pain and unnecessary delays to my destiny. I've learned important lifesaving knowledge from her. She has taught me so much more than how to grow, survive and thrive. She has taught me to be a lifelong student of life, always growing, learning, and changing to become a better person as a result of what I learn. I am forever grateful for her in my life and will always cherish her wisdom, love, generosity, and support.

Do you hold on to the wisdom you have been given by your elders? Do you have a grandmother, grandfather, aunt, uncle, or mentors that have taken the time to share their wisdom with you? Hold onto it as a dear treasure and use it daily to help guide your thinking and decision-making processes.

I know that when we are going through something one of the ways to help yourself is to help others. Helping others can fill our joy tank. When my children were growing up, we frequently went to Atlanta to volunteer with a local church to feed people on Saturday morning. I wanted them to see the benefit of helping others in their life. I got much joy from blessing someone else. I got much joy from my children helping someone else. My joy tank was full when I left because I was able to give back to others. My children have a legacy of giving back to others as well. We are not an island unto ourselves. We are a part of a larger community. At the time, my children didn't like it at all. We have to get up and be there by 6:30 on a Saturday morning. They really didn't like me at that moment. I had a job to do, and that was to show them the importance of being a blessing to others and appreciate your own blessings in return. I felt more connected to my purpose when I was doing something purposeful. My joy was being multiplied because I wasn't focusing on myself.

When we join that community, we join in the brotherhood of helping others. When my oldest son was in college, he regularly volunteered with Habitat for Humanity. He was the president of his college chapter of Habitat for Humanity. Also, He was granted a scholarship that allows him to go to other continents to do volunteer work. He went to Argentina for three weeks to help teach children math and English, and it really changed his life forever. He saw extreme poverty and he saw children, so impoverished, they barely had anything to eat. He came back home a different person. He has always been sweet, kind, and appreciative, but this made him even more appreciative. He was able to impact lives internationally. What a blessing. Also, my younger son is a little league basketball coach. He volunteers and coaches elementary school children. When I'm long gone, and my story is over, my legacy will live on as an outreach for helping others, which in turn helps us.

You are bigger than just you. You are we. You are us. We fulfill me. Think about that. How many of us feel completely okay with living the rest of our lives in isolation? I would think and hope very few. That means your life isn't just about you. Your life is about you and the people around you. I'm not speaking of just your trusted inner circle. I'm talking about the community in which you live. It's all a part of the we community. When we take care of me, we have more for we. Your heart gets so much more fulfillment when it gives to others and nurtures others. That's the way we were designed.

Some of our richest memories come from times we spent with our loved ones or doing something for someone else. Our richest memories seldom come from times spent in self-indulgence. We don't remember the time we bought our Coach bag or Jimmy Choo shoes. We remember sticky kisses from babies. We remember comforting hugs from friends. We remember laughing during a family dinner or cheering our children on at a sporting event. We remember birthday parties with friends and family. We remember staying up all night nursing a sick child back to health. All of these memories are we and not me.

Our soulfulness is tied to we. When we embrace that, we embrace the core of our soulfulness. We embrace a life of joy that can't be taken away unless we give it away. There is a contentment we have as a result of our connectivity to others. Connectivity fills our soul and our hearts, and that's the pathway to our joyfulness.

Do you give it away or keep it? Your joy? Do you give it away or keep it? All too often, we make a decision whether consciously or not to give our joy away. We give it to people who shouldn't even have the power to take it. They may or may not even know they are taking it. Some do, and some don't. Your joy is your responsibility and no one else's. I am guilty of giving my joy away because of wrong relationships. I used to try too hard and care too much. When I ended up being disappointed over and over, I had to look in the mirror and take responsibility for myself. Why was I sad? Why did I lack joy and peace? Did this person do something to me to rob me of it? The actions of the individual may have been negative or wrong, and they may through their negative actions have earned my anger and disappointment, but the reality of the matter is I had a choice to make. At the time my choice was to allow them to control my emotions. I gave away my power. They didn't even know it. They acted, I reacted. I, of course, expressed how I was feeling, and they responded. After the initial conversation, however, I had a choice to make. Maintain my joy or walk around angry and upset. Then I chose the latter, now my choice is to control my own feelings and emotions. I don't allow people to steal what belongs to me. My joy is mine, and I'm going to keep it. Your joy is yours. You can keep it or give it away. There are so many different situations I could name that can rob you of your joy. Maybe you have jealous coworkers whose sole purpose at work is to upset you. Maybe you have children that work your last nerve. Perhaps you have siblings that thrive on bringing drama into the family. Sometimes we are involved in marriages and relationships with people who are not happy with themselves and take it out on you. Your situation could be with the mother or father of your children. Your relationship with them didn't work, so they want to make your life miserable. Do you see yourself in any of these scenarios? Now, you have a choice to make. Now, you can choose to keep or give away your power.

When you recognize a situation that is sapping you of your joy and peace, pray about it. Ask God to help you cope with it until he removes that person from your life or brings you to a place where their actions no longer affect you. Don't worry, nothing is ever permanent. I have learned through my time on Earth, that the only certainty in life is change. Seasons change, and people change. Nothing stays the same forever.

Think about the strategies I gave you earlier. Use those strategies to maintain your peace and joy. If you have a negative coworker, try your best to go to work with peace. No matter what they say or do, maintain that peace. You could listen to positive music before you go to work, pray, read your Bible, meditate, take deep breaths, watch inspirational YouTube videos, talk to a friend or a family member. Read a great book. These are great ways to release stress and maintain your peace. When you leave work, leave the situation there. Don't bring it home with you because then you have given that person power over you.

If you are in a relationship with someone who is not treating you the way you should be treated, let them know. Set the expectations for how you want to be treated. If they don't live up to your standards, have the strength to leave. No one is worth you sacrificing your joy and peace for. I've learned that the hard way. I protect my joy and peace at all costs. So should you. It's more difficult when you are married to that person. If you are married to someone who does not treat you right, I suggest you seek the professional services of a counselor or therapist. This person can help you work through difficult situations. They can help guide you through the process of creating a joy-filled life. You might be in the way of living a joy-filled and peaceful life. Maybe you are not happy with yourself, and you live in the moment. A professional therapist or life coach can help you get back on track. They can help you get to the core of what is holding you back from your soulfulness. They can help you with what's missing in your life and how to fill that void, so you can feel whole and complete again.

Also find someone in your life that can help you become your best you. I have a couple of people in my life that I depend on to help mold me and shape me into the person I am today. I trust them, to be honest with me, chastise me when I'm wrong, celebrate my accomplishments and always give me an unbiased perspective on issues I discuss with them. These are the people who will say, "I disagree with you, and this is why..." At that point, I have an opportunity to go back to my thought process and see, if maybe there was something I was missing. I may change my mind about what I was thinking or what I was going to do or a decision I was about to make. Sometimes, I may agree to disagree with them and continue to make the best decision for me according to my level of understanding and my perspective. I always share my writings with them and my spoken word with them and get their feedback on that as well. Each person should have someone like that in their life. I'm better, stronger, and wiser because of my trusted inner circle, who love me enough to tell me the truth because they know owning my truth will enable me to spread my wings and fly. If you have siblings or family members who are joy robbers, limit your time around them, let them know, you choose not to be around negativity. They will either get on board or stay away. I understand, we cannot choose our family and if we could, some of us would have chosen different people. We can, however, choose who we allow into our life. We can make a choice to not allow into our life people who don't respect us, are abusive to us either verbally, mentally, financially or physically. We can choose not to be around those people and not have those people around us. It sets the tone for every other area of your life.

Once you grasp the fact that you are the one in control of your joy and peace and you possess the power to keep it or let it go, you are changed as a person. You are stronger and more powerful. When people around you notice the change be ready for some resistance from some people. They are not going to be used to the new you, and that's fine. They can either get on board or be left behind. Some people will stay and some will go, and that's okay. It may cost you some relationships with some people and that's okay too. The people who are meant to be will stay, and the ones who are no longer tied to your destiny will leave. Wave goodbye with peace and love in your heart. When the people in your life have a sincere, healthy love for you, they will embrace a positive change in you. They will embrace your joy journey and your desire to feel soulful. They will understand, that as you change and evolve into a more soulful self, it will positively impact your relationship with them. You can bring them on your journey with you, and you can all have abundant joy and an overflow of soulfulness. When they leave bid them well. Reflect on any good they may have brought into your life and forgive them for the bad. It doesn't matter who is or is not on board with you, what matters is that you control the ride and determine the destination. You are an adult, and your life belongs to you.

Your journey will be a collage of color. It will include bright hues of happiness, joy, celebration, and peace. It will include some black and whites, of tough decisions made and doors closed and people leaving. It will have a few gray areas of unfinished business, that may or may not ever truly be finished. Some people will be a bright color of consistency throughout, some will have a small happy space or a small, sad space and these colors will be blends of natural hues, and some will only be seen as a small reflection in the shadows of your life, and that's fine. Be at peace with that. Your joy journey to soulfulness is a journey that is constantly changing and evolving. As you seek to become your best self, you come out of your shell. You walk into your truth with courage. Your truth is personal to you. How you see yourself will change from year to year from decade to decade. During that time you learn more about yourself, and that's when you take your power back. You understand that you have the power to be your best self. Nurture the person you are and are evolving into. Remind yourself of the price you paid to get there. Because when we know our value and appreciate the price paid, we cherish it more and treat it as the rare jewel that it is. Our soulfulness is our strength. We champion the person we are and use it for our good. Champion the person you are. You have been chosen by God. You are created in His image for His purpose. You were uniquely created with certain gifts and attributes, and you are the only person who can bring those gifts and attributes to this world.

God created you just like He did so that your gifts and talents would be unique to you. There are gifts and talents inside of you that only you possess. If you were not born, we would not have your gifts and talents. There were lives that you were created to be a part of. If you were not born, these people would not have you in their lives. You were created to bless certain people, touch certain people, love certain people, give birth to certain people, encourage certain people, educate certain people, and change certain people. You are needed and necessary to so many people for so many different reasons.

The lessons you have learned? Somebody needs you to give them your wisdom. The hugs you give? Someone needs to feel them. They joy in your laughter? Someone needs to hear it. There is someone that needs only the comfort that you provide for them. There are family members that need your love, your presence, your care, and your comfort. If you were not born, not created, and had not persevered and pressed through, there would be something lacking in a lot of people's lives because you are not there.

My children enjoy my cooking, but there are certain things I cook, that they really enjoy more. When I make these dishes, they tell me often, no one makes these dishes like you. No matter how many other people may make the same dish, it's not the same as yours. I told my son one day when he is married, I would give his wife the recipe for my cornbread dressing. He shook his head no! He said, it still won't be yours. I laughed. That comment made me feel really good because in my son's mind and heart no one else in this world could make his mama's homemade cornbread dressing. This is what I mean when I said there are certain things only you can bring to this world that are genuinely needed. You are incredibly special and very necessary. That knowledge alone should bring you joy and help you feel soulful.

CHAPTER 9
A DIAMOND IN THE ROUGH

When seeking to create and maintain a life of joy, you must look at the value in each experience that life brings to you. Our negative experiences are designed to bring out value in us just like our positive experiences. I know it doesn't seem like it, but if you hold on and don't give up, it will one day. It's too difficult to think about when you are in it or have just come out of it. I understand that, and I get that. I'm sure because I've been through several heartbreaking situations myself and each time, I came out of them different than when I went in, and I was stronger as a result.

I think about the beauty of a diamond. As a woman, I do believe diamonds are a girl's best friend or at least makes a girl very happy! I love diamonds because they are so beautiful. They are sparkly and shiny. However, diamonds don't start off that way. How can something found within the dirty ground, bring me so much joy? The reason a diamond is so beautiful is that it is rare and it has endured so much in the formation stages. It has to go from being something found in the rough to something that is transformed into a brilliant sparkling, rare gem that brings people joy to have. The process of changing a diamond from something rough to beautiful and shiny is a tedious process and must be done with precision and much care. It takes time for the transformation to occur. The gemologist must be patient with the process. It is the same thing with any gem of value. It has to go through the process of transformation from its natural stage to its beautiful, brilliant stage. There is always a process involved.

Our lives are the same way. Sometimes we go through a painful process. We lose our job, go through a divorce, go through a depression, file bankruptcy, or lose a loved one. The pain is so deep and so intense, sometimes, we can barely breathe. We literally feel physical pain in our hearts and sometimes body as well because the grief and heartbreak is just too much. Our blood pressure goes up, our hearts start to beat fast, our head begins throbbing, and we feel physically sick. We lose sleep, lose weight, overeat, smoke, drink, or cry. We do anything we can to ease the pain because the pain never feels good. We go through stages and in those stages; we feel deeply whatever feeling we have in our heart at that moment. This is when soul work is so important. It is important to create value in our lives and create joy. The process is when we reach through the pain and reach into ourselves and pull out our peace, purpose, and joy. We go back to what I discussed earlier; those things that make us feel soulful. We pray, meditate, exercise, give back, go through counseling, lean on our support system. It's difficult but necessary.

After we go through this refining process, that's when we find the value in our joy. That's when we hold it dear and treasure it because we know the value of the work that was put into making it what it is. Joy is a rare jewel that is to be valued and treasured because it is so hard to come by. When we do that, other people see the value in our joy as well. That value we hold dear can add value to the lives of other people. We can share our value with them. It's like a man giving his girlfriend a diamond engagement ring. They both know the value of the diamond, so it's special to both of them. It is the symbol of a lifelong commitment. When we share our joy with others, we give them something of value from ourselves to them. If they value us, they value the joy we bring into their lives. We both hold it dear because we know there is a price attached to it and that price is whatever process we had to go through to receive it and give it to them as a gift.

The value you attach to your soulfulness will be evident by the choices you make in life. You can see the value some people place on their soulfulness by the choices they make. The godless acts of people show you're the depravity of their souls and the lack of value they place on their life and on their soul. They hurt themselves and others without regard for the value of human life. People think, how can they do that? Because of the lack of soul work they have done. There is a deficit in their soul, and they don't feel whole, so they seek to hurt themselves and others. They have been swallowed up in a deep dark, soulless black hole and have no value for life, their life or others. They are no longer able to associate with the feelings of pain, empathy, sympathy, or understand the morality of right and wrong.

Joyfulness is found in forgiveness. The most important gift you can give yourself is the gift of forgiveness. Forgiveness is a gift to heal your soul and spirit. It's a gift that lasts a lifetime. Forgiveness helps you move closer to your destiny. It's important to achieving your joyfulness to whitewash your soul. When a white fence gets dirty, you can pressure wash it and then whitewash it to restore the purity of the color to the fence. You can make it pure white again. When I whitewash my soul, I do it to remove the pain, hurt, anger, betrayal, to restore the purity of my soul, once it has been tarnished. I paint my soul with love, joy, peace, and happiness. If your soul has been stained by hurt, betrayal, and disappointment, let God wash your soul in his love, forgive yourself and forgive those who have wronged you. Forgiveness comes when you open your soul to God. He is the one who can fill you with forgiveness of self. He can erase your feelings of guilt and shame. He can fill you with love for yourself despite the mistakes you have made. He can remove the guilt stain of your past. He can whitewash your soul. He can heal you of your pain and heal you of your guilt. He can make your soul clean again and give you the wisdom needed to make the right choices for your life. So you can lead a soulful and joyful life. To do this, you must, understand your relationship with God and spend time with Him.

I encourage you to be purposeful about your joy. Be purposeful about creating it and maintaining it. We all have peaks and valleys in our lives. When we have the valley experience in our lives, it is more important than ever to be selfish enough to put our soul work as a priority in our lives. The hardest thing to do in life is to be purposeful in our life in the middle of pain. When we are in our valley experience, we feel the most vulnerable.

I know several women who have gone through a divorce. I have been told that the experience is heartbreaking. It is the death of a dream. It is the end of hope for that part of your life. I can only imagine that would be a difficult experience to go through especially when the reason for the divorce was some type of abusive behavior. Many women and men leave marriages because of some type of abuse. When you are going through this experience, I can imagine, you would not feel soulful at all.

You are in your Valley experience. An experience, where you feel you are at your lowest. You feel emotionally depleted and insufficient. Ask yourself, what can you do for your soul to feel whole again and to feel joyful? Life is short, live it on purpose in and out of season no matter what you are going through.

Now would be a good time to put in place a time each day to feed your soul, a time to devote to an activity that makes you feel happy, joyful, and less sad. For me, hiking is that thing. I started hiking as a hobby around 2001. I'm a nature lover, and I love the outdoors. I've always enjoyed being around nature. Being around nature makes me feel peaceful. It brings me much joy. Hiking is a spiritual experience for me because I feel and see God in nature. When I lost my husband, I started power walking and hiking, to lose weight and relieve stress. I didn't realize it at the time, but I would come to find that hiking would give me so much more than health benefits.

I would hike early in the morning, and the hike was and still is very difficult for me. As many times as I have been hiking, it has never gotten any easier to get to the top of that mountain. Each time I begin my journey, I always struggle to get to the top. I have to utilize all of my fortitudes to make it to the top. Most times I hike alone, so I bring music with me to help me make it to the top. However difficult the journey, though I always enjoy the scenery on my way up to the top. It is an absolutely beautiful journey to the top. The views are amazing. Sometimes I stop along the way just to admire the views. I've taken several pictures throughout the years. Sometimes, I see deer, rabbits, snakes, and squirrels. It's such a beautiful place. As difficult as the journey is, however, it brings me great satisfaction and peace.

I hike to the top, and at the top, there is a spot I like to go to. It's my secret place. That's the place I can go to and feed my soul. That's the place that gives me the most joy. When I get to the top, I feel soulful. I feel joyful. I can go and pray, meditate, think, hope, reflect, distress, plan, dream, and get my happy back. When I'm at the top of the mountain in my secret place that is when I feel closest to God.

When I sit there and look at the amazing view and inhale and exhale, I feel like I am most connected to God in that space. I feel like it's just God there and me. We are having a special time of communication, and He is empowering me. I let all of my stress go. I let all of my hurts and disappointments go. I let go of all of the mistakes I have made, so many of my dreams were born on that mountain. So much of my emotional healing has come on top of that mountain. So much strength has been received on top of that mountain. I literally come down a different person. I don't care how many people are around, at that moment, I feel like it's just God and me. I feel such a sense of accomplishment to have made it to the top. For me, it's a little slice of heaven right here on earth.

Since I enjoy hiking so much, I go year round when the weather permits. I've been hiking in the spring, summer, winter, and fall. My least favorite time is the winter because it's so cold. I'm not a cold weather lover. However, God showed me so much when I went there in the winter time. In the winter time, all of the trees are bare. They have lost all of their leaves. The beauty of spring and fall colors are gone, and everything is lying dormant.

One day as I was hiking up the mountain, I noticed the absence of the colors because of the season. God showed me something. When the trees lost their leaves, they did not change. When the seasons changed, they remained the same. They had lost their leaves, but if you notice, that even when a tree loses its leaves, it posture remains the same. Its branches are always facing upward. It's like they are in a posture of praise. The branches don't change their posture when they lose their leaves. No matter how cold it gets, no matter how many leaves it loses, no matter how the weather changes, the posture of the tree remains the same. Its branches are always pointed upward. The branches of the tree pointing upward are to me a posture of praise. It's a posture of surrender and praise. It symbolizes to me, the trees praising God in and out of season and just being thankful to exist.

Thinking of that revelation, I thought to myself, what if that was me? What if I were like the tree? What if no matter what season of my life I was in, I had a posture of praise? During my Spring I have new ideas, a new season of favor, new blessings, new friends, new relationships, and new beginnings. In my Summer everything is warm and beautiful, finances, family, career, and health are all in full bloom. My Fall brings the changing of relationships, changing of family life, finances, and aging. My Winter brings the death of a loved one, loss of a job, loss of finances, difficulty with children, loss of joy, purpose, or vision. What If I consistently maintain an attitude of praise? What if I am just like the tree and remain joyful, hopeful, soulful, and grateful to simply have life and to exist? How would that impact my life and the lives of the people around me? The trees gave me food for thought and something to strive towards.

I want to be just that joyful in every season in my life because my time on this earth is brief and I want to live and love in each moment. I want to have a posture of praise and be thankful for the opportunity to exist and have a life regardless of the season in life I may be in. I don't compare myself with others because I have no idea what their journey is all about and what they have had to go through to get there. I focus on me, and I run my own race. That keeps me focused on what I need to do for me.

To maintain your joy, you must never spend time dwelling on what people think of you. What people think of you is none of your business. It robs you of the time thinking of what you need to do for yourself. Let their opinions roll off of you and keep it moving. Let them deal with that. It's their issue, so don't make it yours.

That is what I challenge myself to do. I challenge myself to find joy on a daily basis. Joy is my choice each day. Do I accomplish my goal every day? No, but if I make a conscious decision each day to find joy, I will have a much richer and fuller life as a result. I am not a joy expert. I am sharing with you things I have learned over the years that have been helpful to me and others around me. I remind myself each day, I am powerful and not powerless. My actions alone determine my level of soulfulness and not the actions of others around me. I want to laugh often, love hard, forgive quickly, but never lose the lessons I have learned and allow people the opportunity to earn my trust. I have too much to live for to slow down now and lose valuable time. I don't know how much time, I will be given, but I will maximize all the time I am given.

CHAPTER 10
THE POWER OF DISCIPLINE

Another key element, important for us to have joy abundantly, we must exercise discipline. This is why God calls us disciples. We are to be of the mindset that we are students on a daily journey to learn and apply biblical truth to our lives. Soulfulness is not a destination. It is a daily journey of self-discovery, sacrifice, and discipline. The discipline part comes into play when we deny or forgo our temporary desires for a more fulfilling purpose later on. It takes that understanding to be in our most peaceful place.

I want your joy journey to include your mind, body, and soul. Are you taking care of your body? Are you giving your body healthy fuel to keep it going, so it can take care of you when you are older? There are many instances when people are very ill, through no fault of their own. Those are not the people I'm referring to. I'm referring to people who abuse their bodies with unhealthy choices on a daily basis. My mom has high blood pressure, and my dad was a diabetic. I'm predisposed genetically to having high blood pressure and diabetes. Each choice I make about my body will impact me either positively or negatively. I choose life. I want to have a long life. I want to have a long healthy life. I don't believe it is my destiny to have high blood pressure or diabetes, so I will care for my temple very carefully and make taking care of it, my highest priority.

The number one killer of women is heart disease. Why? Because we as women are nurturers by nature and we care for everyone except ourselves. We care for parents, children, spouses, and other family members and even friends. We are always so busy with others, we are neglecting ourselves. We work, cook, clean, do laundry, take care of the family, etc., The list never ends. When do we make the time to care for us? We think we don't have time, but we really do. It's totally OK to be selfish with your time to take care of yourself. We have to realize something very important. We master time, time doesn't master us. What I mean by that is, we decide what we do with the time we have. If we are blessed to wake up each day, we are given 24 hours in that day. What we do with that 24 hours, is up to us. I get up at 4:50 A.M. every day to go to the gym to work out. It's really difficult to do, but time doesn't master me, I master time. I choose each day, to make my health a priority. I take time for me on a consistent basis because that allows me to be the best I can be for everyone else.

I spoke with my physician. She said, Shoner, you need to lose weight. You are overweight. You need to lose 15 pounds. I already knew what she was saying was true. So, I made a decision to lose 15 pounds. I knew the benefits of losing weight would allow me to be healthy and have a long life. I decided long life was important to me, so I did something about it. I started running again. It was hard in the beginning, and the weather was cold, but I did it. I ran and walked some. I wanted to reach my weight loss goal and be an example to others of what they can do as well. I'm now up to running four miles at a time. I ran a little more each time. I had a strong desire to do it, so during my running when I wanted to quit, I would just tell myself, you can do it, just a few more steps. When I would see that I had run two miles, I would say, ok, you are half way there. The rest is doable. I would pray, think, meditate, or listen to music. I did whatever I could to encourage myself. I knew I could because I had done it before and I was able to run 6.2 miles. I just had to build myself back up again. It's just a matter of making the time and having the desire to do it. We make time for what's important. I cherish the body God gave me and my desire is to be a good steward of it. Each day we are given is God's way of saying; here is a do-over, get it right. I'm thankful for that. Are you thankful? Do you show your gratitude by being a good steward? No excuses. Your body is your temple. Treat your temple well. Your body is your best asset. It needs fuel, love, care, and rest to function at full capacity. Whatever you put in, is what you will get out. If you put premium fuel in, through healthy lifestyle choices, you will get premium results back. Going to the doctor for regular checkups and taking multivitamins is important in taking care of your body. Making sure you take time for necessary rest is also important. My friends kid me all the time and say, I can't call you after ten PM because you are already in the bed asleep. They are right. I get up at 4:50 in the morning and I work long days, so going to bed on time is important to me. I also take power naps some days to refuel my body.

Power naps can be very healthy for you in allowing your body the rest it needs to run at full capacity. Getting adequate sleep will keep you looking young and refreshed and not tired and worn down. Don't we all want to look young and refreshed? Your body is a reflection of how much you love and care for yourself. It's an outward expression of an inner manifestation. If there is a health issue, it's ok. Go to the doctor and seek help in getting your body right. I know people who have surgery to lose weight. They get medical help along with a lifestyle change, and it works for them, and they can lead happier more productive lives as a result. Weight Watchers is a great support group for losing weight. I've used Weight Watchers, and it definitely worked for me. I became aware and learned how to make healthy lifestyle choices and how to use food as a fuel for my body. I learned about the importance of keeping my body hydrated with plenty of water. Our body is mostly water, and we need to fuel it with plenty of water. Sometimes we feel tired because we are dehydrated and in need of water for our body. So hydrate your body often and daily. Hydrating yourself cleans your body of toxins, increases your energy level, and gives a boost to the elasticity of your skin. Don't we all want beautiful skin? I learned how to not overeat and how to exercise to help build up my muscle mass in my body to have a healthy, lean, body. I learned to eat more foods that grow on trees and plants, and eat less food that is manufactured in plants. My body has to take me far. I want to live to be 100 and be healthy, happy, and in my right mind. Your mind, body, and soul are all connected. When you take care of one, you take care of the other. So, when your mind and body are healthy, it is better for your soul. Your soul is your spiritual center and life point. This is where your fullness of joy comes from, and this is where your purpose comes from. Give them all the love and care you can and make doing that a priority in your life. Make the time for you each day. No one can do that, but you.

My book is designed for you to have all of those things working a maximum capacity for you to have your maximum life. Don't you want to live a maximum life? Do I have a life of maximum health, joy, love, peace, healing, and wholeness? Each day that is my goal, and that's why I want you to have the knowledge and tools to navigate your life and realize your potential. The most important part is that you are aware of when you do master your life and when you don't, so you can identify what is deterring you and get back on track to where you want to be. As I mentioned earlier, that comes from knowing self. To thine own self, be true, and you cannot be true to a self you don't know. You are your most important gift. Cherish all that you are and all that you have to give to others. You and you alone determine your value. Soulfulness drives your destiny, it drives your favor, it releases God's supernatural power in your life.

This joy that I have has released unmerited favor in my life. Things I was supposed to never have, I have received, from cars, a house, and money, to healing, breakthroughs, and peace. It never fails to happen. God's supernatural favor follows me everywhere I go. It's the joy inside of me showing my gratitude to God for all He has done. I practice praise, and my praise releases my favor. When praises go up, blessings come down. Praise from a pure heart and praise often. When you feel down, put a praise on it. When you feel discouraged, put a praise on it. When you feel defeated, put a praise on it. Watch the very atmosphere change all around you and feel the burden lifted and your heart feels lighter. I dare you to praise in your situation right now! I have allowed His power to fill me, and I'm free as a result. You too can and will be free. Are you ready for all the joy your heart, mind, and soul can embrace? Great! Put a praise on it!

EPILOGUE

My goal in writing this book is to help you find the healing that I have found in my journey to a joy-filled life and feeling soulful. I'm navigating my life in a way that will help others live their best life. Your life matters and your soulfulness matters as well. I want to see you live your best life and understand through your darkness, there is light. Through your bare places, there is light. Through your broken places there is light. In your disappointed places, there is light. Through your valley and on top of your mountain there is light all around you. Be a seeker of the light and that light will find you and give you all of the joy you can stand.

Another chance

I would have fainted lest I believe to see

God's goodness and mercy stretched out for me.

He covered my sins and removed my pain

Gave me hope and unloosed my chains

The darkest of black the darkest of night

My soul was lost far away from the light

Judged by most given up by some

Who could help this wretch undone

Your mistakes will send you straight to the grave

All hope is lost you can't be saved

What makes you think you're the chosen one?

Picked by God the day you were born

Your sins your mistakes negated your destiny

Why do you think you're still blessed to be

An example for the lost depressed and stressed?

I know I am you don't know

That lonely hour when He saved my soul

Filled my soul and soothed my pain

Felt his glory shining again

Change my life, my mind, my soul,

Made me a wonder to behold

Placed all of my talents and gifts in my heart

Said go for my child here is your brand-new start

I have placed inside of you courage and bravery

You need to go forward to fulfill your destiny

Do not be afraid for with you I go

To educate, encourage, and empower each and every lost soul

Let your light shine, and all will see

The God of your righteousness and know they too can be
redeemed

Now my joy is complete my soul is at peace

My trials didn't break me but set me free

Free to live free indeed

In my joy and my destiny

May you have all of the joy your heart can stand!

Positively,

Shoner

AFTERWORD

A sucker punch to the stomach. Right below the belt. It hurts, and it knocks you back a little. It's painful. It's unexpected. It should not be unexpected though because you are in a boxing match fighting for your life. That was my mom. In a boxing match with colon cancer fighting for her life. She was a young, vibrant 78-year-old woman. She was the life of the party when she walked in the room. Then one day she got the call that the mass in her stomach was cancerous and she would need to start chemo right away. For two years and two months, she fought a really good fight.

However, when I got the phone call telling me she had died peacefully in her sleep, I felt like someone had punched me in the gut. I wasn't ready. I wasn't prepared. I wasn't ready to let go. My mom, my mentor, role model, life coach, and my strength had left this world. It felt and still feels surreal. The timing was especially difficult for me because of the same exact weekend, on a Sunday, while I was in church, my late husband passed away sixteen years ago. What are the chances that my mom would pass away sixteen years later on the same exact weekend on the same exact Sunday morning of my late husband? It was too much to wrap my mind around. Before my mom's passing Christmas had always been an especially difficult time of year for me because my late husband had passed away two weeks before Christmas. Then to have my mom pass away at the exact same time of year is a big, bitter, pill for me to swallow.

Here I am anticipating the release of this book, *This Joy That I Have: Life After the Storm*, which was intended to be a reflection of my life after my husband passed away. I had no idea at the beginning of this journey, I would lose my mom as well. Now, I write this as I ponder losing my father, husband, and now my mother. Although, I am blessed to have my children in my life, it is quite different. It's a feeling of being completely alone.

When I was 22, I lost my dad, but I had just met my soon to be husband, and I had my mom. When my husband passed, I still had my mom. Now, that I just found out my mom passed away, it's a completely different feeling. As I write this to encourage you, my prevailing thought is a reflection of one of the many conversations I had with my mother. She walked the journey with me as I wrote this book and she and I had many conversations about the book. She was my inspiration for the chapter on wisdom. She told me often, "Shoner, put yourself out there. You can do it! I believe in you! No one knows where you live, you have to just step out in faith and go be great!"

So... with my mother's approval, God's ordaining, and passion in my heart, I will allow all of my pain to be used to help others become educated, equipped, and empowered to live their best life. *This Joy that I Have* is not about getting to the ultimate place of joy. It is a guide to help you on your journey to create and maintain soulfulness and joy as you live a life of purpose in spite of your circumstances. Your purpose is what is going to bring you to a place of joy because you find that something inside of you that is greater than you and gives your life meaning.

At this moment, my heart is sad, but my soul is at peace. I am embracing joy because my mother fought the good fight and finished her race. She has earned her reward. It is now, my time to honor her legacy by pressing toward the mark of the high calling, which is in Christ Jesus to encourage, uplift, and empower others to live their greatest life with joy.

CPSIA information can be obtained
at www.ICGtesting.com
Printed in the USA
FFOW03n1226031117
41729FF